woodworking
in a weekend

woodworking
in a weekend

20 SIMPLE PROJECTS FOR THE HOME

MARK GRIFFITHS

CHRONICLE BOOKS
SAN FRANCISCO

DEDICATION
*To my wife Gilly, and my
children Amy and Hunter.*

First published in the United States of America
in 2013 by Chronicle Books LLC.

Library of Congress Cataloging-in-Publication
Data available.

ISBN: 978-1-4521-2586-2

Manufactured in China

Text by Mark Griffiths
Designer Naomi MacDougall
Illustrations by Mark Hall-Patch
& John Woodcock
Photography by Neal Grundy
& Andrew Perris

The copyright holder would like to thank
the Brighton & Hove Wood Recycling Project,
the Secret Campsite, the Tin Tabernacle, and
Sian and Chris Wilkings for their assistance
with the photoshoot.

This book was conceived, designed,
and produced by Ivy Press
210 High Street, Lewes
East Sussex BN7 2NS, UK

10 9 8 7 6 5 4 3 2 1

Chronicle Books LLC
680 Second Street
San Francisco, CA 94107
www.chroniclebooks.com

Contents

INTRODUCTION

MANY OF US SHARE A LOVE OF HANDICRAFTS. Even if we feel we personally have no creative talent ourselves, our appreciation of pieces handmade by others is evident in the countless craft stores and fairs across the country. Keeping this in mind, the aim of this book is to present woodworking projects that are achievable by anyone, whatever you think of your woodworking ability. Some of these projects will present their challenges, but working through them is guaranteed to bring you a warm glow of achievement as you stand back to look at the finished results. Nothing beats the sense of pride felt when sitting in a chair or eating from a table you have made yourself.

One of the main reasons we often hold back from unleashing the toolbox is simply the feeling of being out of his or her depth. When it comes to woodworking, just taking a trip to the local lumberyard for wood can be an intimidating experience for the beginner. As much as possible, the projects in this book have been developed to use found and reclaimed lumber, thereby bypassing the lumberyard manned by experts. And because the wood being used is inexpensive—or better yet, free—there's little need to worry about the cost of making mistakes. Also with the intention of keeping expenses down, the projects can also be assembled with a minimum of tools.

The projects I have created in this book have largely taken their form, design, and proportion from the salvaged materials available to me. In a similar fashion, the furniture you create will reflect the reclaimed lumber that you find. This is the beauty of working in this way: each item made is individual and unique to the maker.

Building custom-made and beautiful items for the yard is a great place to begin experimenting with woodworking. You are creating objects that are both practical and great to look at—and that are one of a kind. Using the projects in this book, you will discover a whole new way of looking at and working with wood, and they may even unleash creative talents you didn't know you had. I like to think of the projects contained in this book as an outline or point of reference—they are simply a suggestion for what you can create from materials seen as worthless by others. My hope is that you will be inspired to create new designs and have new ideas as your confidence in making grows.

WHERE TO FIND THE WOOD

It's only when you start salvaging wood to make stuff, that you become aware of just how much useful material most people simply throw away. Finding inexpensive, or even free, lumber that will be great to work with is relatively easy. Here are a few pointers to get you started.

PREPARING YOUR SHOPPING LIST

I've included lumber cutting guides for each project so you can see what I used, but you should adapt the lists to match the reclaimed lumber you find rather than trying to match my materials.

THE SEARCH BEGINS

When it comes to reclaiming wood for these projects, it often helps if you start by gradually building up a stock of items. Each time you happen to be near a yard sale, garage sale, junkyard, salvage center, or flea market, stop and rummage around if time permits. These are all great places to find a bargain, either to break apart for the wood, or convert and reimagine into something else that fits your needs. Even wood crates or pallets used for delivery can be turned into interesting woodworking projects.

It can be intimidating to knock at the door of a woodworking company, such as a carpentry or cabinetmaking workshop, but if you approach with a casual, friendly manner, you can strike up a relationship that may be a source for scrap wood, sheets of manufactured wood, and even advice.

If you have the confidence to visit woodworking workshops, the next step is to visit a construction site. This is a place rich in raw materials that would only be consigned to the Dumpster. Again, it's the right approach that will yield the best rewards. There will be strict on-site health and safety rules, so don't just wander in. Instead, get the attention of whomever is in charge and talk to that person about what you need for your project.

Internet forums can help you to find sources for inexpensive lumber and tools for sale as well as people who can provide helpful advice.

LEFT *In addition to being good for the environment, salvage centers selling reclaimed lumber offer a wide range of different types of wood in a variety of finishes.*

ABOVE LEFT *Softwoods are relatively inexpensive and easy to work with, making them a popular choice for furniture, particularly when you are starting out.*

ABOVE RIGHT *Hardwoods are a viable choice for more experienced woodworkers who want to make a strong impression with their project's final finish.*

Finally, put the word out to family, friends, and neighbors that you are in the market for odd scraps of wood and old furniture that they may no longer have any use for. You will be amazed at the number of people who have what they see as useless junk cluttering up their homes, which they will often gladly donate to your projects.

As a rule, I always have my "breaking kit"—a screwdriver, claw hammer, and handsaw—in the back of the pickup truck, because you never know when you may stumble upon a treasure trove of wood. At times, in fact, I think the search for materials is just as much fun as turning them into something useful.

UNDERSTANDING TYPES OF WOOD

It's a good idea to have a little knowledge about the types of wood before setting out on the hunt. Solid wood is categorized as either softwood or hardwood. Generally, softwood is produced by fast-growing coniferous, or cone-bearing, evergreen trees, such as cedar, Douglas fir, pine, and redwood. It tends to be less stable than hardwood—more prone to movement—when passed through the sawmill and during project making. Typically, there is a greater proportion of knots in softwood than hardwood, and the resinous grain structure of softwood makes it less able to take an even wood stain finish. In its favor, it is easy to work and, with the exception of redwood, inexpensive.

In contrast, hardwood is taken from deciduous, slow-growing, broad-leaved trees. Some of the more common ones used for making furniture are oak, ash, beech, poplar, and cherry. The long growth pattern of this lumber make it more stable when sawed. Along with a good ability to take stain and wood finishes, its tight grain structure can produce beautiful wood patterns. The cons of hardwood are that it is expensive, it weighs a lot, and the tight grain can make it difficult to use screws and nails.

Determining the species of lumber you have sourced is never an easy task because no two pieces of wood are the same, and even seasoned woodworking folk will sometimes be stumped. However, knowing what you have, and how best to use it, can be helpful. Try one of the many online lumber information sites for help with identifying the species.

PROFESSIONAL HELP

At times, a project may require a certain lumber size that is not to be found in your salvaged stock, and there's no other option but to make a trip to your local lumberyard. Some people can find this a little intimidating, and sometimes the staff isn't helpful, shooting technical questions at you about your order. The way to deal with this is to be well prepared, have a list of exactly what you need, take a tape measure to both check sizes and look like a pro, and, finally, don't be afraid to ask for advice. Most lumber is machined to standard stock sizes. Softwood is generally sold by nominal size, which is the size before the wood has been planed, so the actual thickness may be ¼ in/6 mm to ¾ in/ 20 mm smaller in thickness and width. Planed hardwood is about ¼ in/6 mm thinner than its nominal size. Have a look at the lumberyard's website to see the stock sizes it holds, and from this draw up a detailed shopping list.

SALVAGE AND REUSE

Working with salvaged wood is much easier than dealing with lumberyards, and, of course, far more economical. Reclaimed wood will be seasoned; that is, its moisture content will be stable because it has

FAR LEFT *Reclaimed wood will probably be irregular in size, so take your tape measure when you are out to make sure the lumber will be suitable for your project.*

LEFT *Sometimes I find that just browsing in junkyards, flea markets, and similar places will yield unusual pieces that can inspire me to create a new project.*

been around for some time—and a stable moisture content means stable lumber.

There are a few downsides to working with salvaged lumber. One is the possibility that a finish, either paint or varnish, has already been applied to the wood and you don't particularly like it. Faced with this inconvenience, I would always suggest that the best way forward is to first make your project, and then tackle the old finish issue when the piece is together. Working this way, you will avoid spending time and effort removing old finish from wood that either will not be used or won't be seen. Also, a more uniform appearance will be achieved if all the finishing processes are carried out with the item of furniture complete.

Don't be tempted to remove old unwanted finishes with just sandpaper. No matter how coarse the grit, all that will happen is the sandpaper will soon be clogged with a sticky finish residue, costing you time and tons of sandpaper, and it can also reduce the life of your electric sander if you use one. The best approach is to start off by removing as much as you can of the old finish with one of the many chemical paint removers on the market. The chemicals will remove the bulk of the old finish, leaving the job of sanding a far easier task. Due to their toxic nature, you need to be careful when working with these paint removers: wear both eye and hand protection, work in a well-ventilated area, and always read through the manufacturer's instructions before getting started.

THE EXTRAS—THE GOOD AND THE BAD

By their very nature, the majority of reclaimed materials will come accompanied by a host of foreign bodies, some of which will be welcomed, such as old handles and hinges. Over the years, I have amassed enough handles, hinges, and fittings to open my own hardware store. These are a great resource for my projects, and for friends needing to replace or renew. However,

on the downside, old wood can also be home to a lot of old rusted nails and screws, and, if you are really unlucky, any number of wood-boring insects.

Screws and nails will be relatively easy to remove with the claw of your trusty claw hammer. If the odd nail snaps flush with the surface as you attempt to yank it out of the wood, place a thick, new nail over the end of the submerged broken one and give it a sharp tap with the hammer. This should knock the old nail out far enough to grab it.

Unfortunately, wood-boring insects are not as straightforward as nails to deal with. Although there are many chemical treatments on the market aimed at eliminating these pests, I would personally recommend not using the wood at all, if possible. Why risk introducing one of these troublesome beasts into your home?

BELOW *The nature of reclaimed wood will mean you may find nails and other objects in the wood that will need to be removed before you start on your project.*

THE TOOLBOX

Each project in this book has been designed so that only a basic tool kit will be necessary. The idea is to get you to try your hand at woodworking—without spending too much on materials or equipment—so that you get a feeling for it and can see if it's something you would like to continue to do.

SECONDHAND BARGAINS

The basic tools you will need are easy to find and relatively inexpensive to buy. However, before you head off to the local hardware store with a tool list in hand, start your tool hunt at a yard sale, secondhand store, or one of the reuse centers that are springing up around the country. By searching around in these places, you will discover once-loved tools ready to do service again, and they are often sold at a fraction of the cost of their shiny new counterparts.

As an avid collector of woodworking tools, I can tell you that in my opinion these old faithfuls are every bit as good as or, in many cases, far superior to new items. There is also the immense satisfaction to be achieved from putting together your own tool kit from items you have discovered discarded in a box of junk, taken the time to clean up, and then used to create your own furniture. Also take the time to mention your new interest in woodworking to family and friends, who may have old unused tools rusting away in a garage or basement. Many of the tools in my collection have been passed on to me, and their previous owners have been glad to see them enthusiastically put back to use once again.

THE HANDSAW

When starting out, the only tool from the basic kit I would suggest buying new is a handsaw. Although often to be found among collections of old tools, it is rare to find a handsaw that is sharp. The teeth on old handsaws can be sharpened, but

LEFT *The backs of some handsaws come with marks to aid drawing 45- and 90-degree angles.*

it is a skill that takes time to learn. A sharp saw is essential for the projects in this book—for that matter, most woodworking projects—because blunt teeth can make using the saw more difficult and more dangerous. I recommend picking up a general all-round handsaw with a 20-in/51-cm blade that has 11 tpi, or teeth per inch—and also look for one that has a handle designed to mark both 45- and 90-degree angles.

MOVING BEYOND THE BASIC KIT

Although the basic tool kit will get the job done, those called out in the "for an easy life" list at right will take some of the hard work out of the process. Some woodworking tasks can be long, repetitive, and a little boring, and these few additional tools will speed things along, taking some of the tedium out of certain tasks.

Inevitably, as your interest in woodworking grows, the benefits of expanding the range of tools on hand will be obvious. Not only will that newly acquired jigsaw speed up cutting time, but it will

Hole saw

Handsaw

Screwdriver, Phillips and flat-head

Hand drill

Pliers

Claw hammer

Tape measure

¾-in/2-cm chisel

Set of drill bits

Clamp

Electric sander

Wood rasp, half round and flat

Cordless drill/driver

Carpenter's pencil *

Jigsaw

Surform plane

*A carpenter's pencil has a thick, square lead, which produces a strong line that is still visible when covered in sawdust, and it won't keep breaking if marking on rough grain, so one is well worth the investment.

THE BASICS

Handsaw

Hole saw

Tape measure

Screwdrivers, Phillips and flat-head

Hand drill and drill bits

Claw hammer

Carpenter's pencil

Wood rasp

Surform plane

Clamp

Pliers

Chisel

FOR AN EASY LIFE

Electric sander

Cordless drill/driver

Jigsaw

also take the design possibilities you have to new levels. Suddenly boring straight lines become seductive curves, plain flat panels can be adorned with fretwork, and work that previously took hours now takes minutes.

When it takes hold, collecting tools can almost become an obsession. This is more the case with old and antique woodworking tools; there is just something about these well-worn, well-loved pieces that inspires us to put them back to work and carry on where the last owner left off. Many of the secondhand chisels I own have the name of at least two previous craftsmen stamped into their honey-color wood handles. And I'm sure from my hand they will pass along to the next maker in

line. By investing in previously owned tools, you have the opportunity to restore and rejuvenate. It will take a little research and investigation to discover how the tool needs to be set, sharpened, or just held when working, and during this process your knowledge of the craft will grow.

COMMUNITY TOOLS

For anybody just starting out who may find their enthusiasm to make tempered only by a lack of equipment and a lack of funds, I would recommend joining a neighborhood tool-sharing project. If there isn't one in your neighborhood, then why not start one yourself? A tool-sharing project offers a fantastic opportunity to meet up with other eager woodworkers, and to save money by pooling your resources. Community organizations can also be a source of advice, physical help when an extra pair of hands is needed, material swapping, or just friendship based in a common interest. The sharing group I'm part of gets together for a big barbecue once a month, which is an opportunity to talk about the projects we're working on at the moment, to get advice on anything wood related, and to show off new equipment and tools people have acquired. They are also loads of fun.

CARING FOR YOUR TOOLS

As you spend your weekends creating woodworking projects and developing your skills, all the while adding to and building up a cherished collection of tools, the need to properly store and care for them will become apparent. Whether old or new, a tool collection will represent a financial investment that is worth protecting. If you are lucky enough to have a dedicated workshop or working space, storage should be a straightforward matter. If possible, keep the majority of your collection stored on racks, shelves, or hung from hooks on a wall so that you will have quick access to them. If hidden out of sight, it's much too easy to forget what you have.

How your workshop is set up is important; for example, a damp atmosphere will cause metal tools to rust and wooden handles to warp. If dampness is an issue, you could install a dehumidifier, which will also benefit your stack of lumber.

If the idea of a dedicated workshop decked out with racks of tools is just a dream rather than reality, it is still important that your precious tool collection is well cared for. Investing in a good-quality toolbox is essential. In many households, the tool collection can be found dumped together in an old box in a cupboard or rattling around in a bottom drawer. If you want your tools to work for you, you have to show them some respect. As well as housing your collection in neat, easy-to-see compartments, a toolbox will give you the opportunity to transport your kit to wherever the work takes you. Not only do many toolboxes on the market today offer waterproof storage, but some also allow you to use the top as a small work station, which is perfect for the woodworker with space constraints.

Whether storing your tools on racks, shelves, or in a toolbox, it's important to make sure that any sharp edges have been covered with some form of protection—many people have cut their fingers when removing uncovered, sharp tools from a toolbox before they've even started their woodwork. Most hardware stores sell a selection of dedicated plastic blade guards or tool rolls.

PURCHASING POWER TOOLS

Picking up and maintaining hand tools is a fairly simple pursuit, but acquiring power tools is a little more complicated. If you are buying them brand new—which, if the budget can stretch to it, is what I recommend—do as much research as possible before making your purchase. Check online review sites, which are often a helpful source of information, and ask any tradespeople you may know if they have any recommendations.

LEFT *Jigsaws, electric drill/drivers, and power sanders aren't essential, but they are useful.*

OPPOSITE *Top-quality hand tools can become heirlooms, handed down through generations.*

A decent hardware store will have knowledgeable staff who are helpful and who are familiar with all the different products on the market. They should point you in the direction of the right power tool to suit your needs.

I tend to discourage people from purchasing secondhand electric tools. I know that the majority of woodworkers, like myself, will only be done with a power tool either after they have squeezed the best years of life out of it or the motor has fried. If, however, you do come across a tool that appears to be in good condition and at a price that can't be ignored, buy it, but do have it serviced by a registered power-tool technician before you use it. This shouldn't cost much and, for safety reasons, is essential.

Hopefully, the list on page 13 will give you guidance if you happen to be starting out and putting together your first set of tools. As you make progress with the different projects on these pages, I hope that your interest in working with wood will grow, along with your passion for building up your own tool collection.

YOUR WORKING SPACE

Setting up a working space correctly is important to make sure you work safely, and it will help you work more efficiently and easily. A well-organized workshop makes woodworking a more enjoyable—and safe—experience. Here are a few tips to get you started.

SETTING UP

Before starting out on your first project, you will need to set up a working space. In an ideal world, this would be based around a good and sturdy workbench, decked out with strong vises. More realistically, the novice woodworker will be making do with an old table, a pair of sawhorses, or a folding workbench. These last options will work fine just as long as you also use some form of clamps to secure the work in place.

It's essential to be sure that wherever you plan to work, the location has a strong light source, even if it means working outside in the sunshine. Decent light will put a clear perspective on what you are doing and, hopefully, help you to avoid missing a vital pencil mark.

LUMBER

Every plank of lumber is different, and you want to make sure the piece you use is of the best quality for the job at hand. Check each plank over for any large knots or splits that may affect its strength. Then line your eye along its length, as if you were sighting a rifle; doing this will highlight if the lumber stock is bowed or warped in any way.

HAND TOOLS

Each tool in your toolbox comes with its own little idiosyncrasies. When using your claw hammer, for example, get into the habit of holding it close to the end of the handle to give the head more striking power. Also, if you find the nails you are driving in have a tendency to bend over, try rubbing the face

FAR LEFT *When buying lumber, check along the length of each board for small irregularities.*

LEFT *Applying a small amount of wax to a screw can make it easier to drive it in.*

GETTING THE KIDS INVOLVED

When your children reach a suitable age, woodworking is a great activity to enjoy with them. Start by picking up a few safe tools and a little box for your children while you build your own collection. Each of my two children has their own toolbox filled with a collection of nondangerous items, such as screwdrivers, small hammers, and pieces of sandpaper, and it's a joy to watch how involved they become when helping out on a project. Starting children off in this way, with a hands-on appreciation and understanding of how things go together, will give them the confidence to take on their own creative projects as they grow. Having worked with tools from an early age, children naturally mature with a good sense of self-reliance and respect for the craft of woodworking.

of the hammer on a piece of sandpaper until shiny; this will help stop the nail from bending by removing pits or rust that can cause the face of the hammer to deflect.

If you have invested in a sharp handsaw, it should cut through material with relative ease. If, however, the saw seems to be sticking, rub either a candle or beeswax on the blade to help it ease through the work.

When cutting, let the saw do the work to help keep the saw on the pencil marks you want it to follow—avoid the temptation to force the saw through, which will probably make it waiver from those marks.

Regularly check the heads of your screwdrivers; if worn or of inferior quality, the lack of crispness of the tips will affect their ability to drive home a screw without the screwdriver slipping or damaging the screw head. Like the saw, applying a small amount of wax to a screw will help when fitting.

SCREWS AND NAILS

Given the choice, I will always stretch the budget to get the best screws and nails I can. It can be very demoralizing when assembling a project to find you are up against low-quality screws that become stripped and break at every step.

CORDLESS DRILL/DRIVER

If you are fortunate enough to have a cordless drill/driver for driving screws, be sure to take advantage of the speed controls and torque settings. A slower speed setting will offer greater control when driving in screws and, for that matter, when making holes with larger drill bits. Using a lower torque setting will help avoid the inconvenience of screw heads becoming stripped, or being sheared off altogether.

When investing in drill bits, pick up a set with a lip and spur cutting tip. These will give you a crisp, more accurate hole when drilling into wood. They should only be used on wood to ensure a long life.

SAFETY

There will always be an element of risk when using hand or power tools. The chances of any injury will be greatly reduced if the woodworker follows these simple safety rules.

- Always wear suitable safety gear, such as eye goggles, heavy-duty gloves, and a dust mask.

- Make sure the work is securely held in place before starting any operation.

- Keep the working area clear of debris or any item that could cause an obstruction.

- Always keep hands behind any sharp power or hand tool, and make sure that as you use a tool, it is never directed toward a hand, leg, or other body part.

- Don't put yourself or anybody else in what could be a potentially dangerous situation.

- Use ground fault circuit interrupters (GFCI) and be aware of the cords when using power tools.

- Always follow the manufacturer's advice when using products.

JIGSAW

Using a jigsaw for the first time can be a daunting prospect; however, if you follow the basic rules—secure the workpiece firmly on a workbench, always keep fingers and cords well away from the blade, and read the manufacturer's instructions—you will find the jigsaw an incredibly versatile tool. Most jigsaws have a blade that cuts with a pendulum motion. A control switch on the saw will allow you to change the pendulum pitch; for example, a low setting works well on thin boards, whereas a higher pitch will give the saw a more aggressive cut suitable for thicker material. Invest in the range of blades available for cutting different materials to get the most from your jigsaw. As with the handsaw, you should never put pressure on the jigsaw, which will just send it off course.

A mistake that is often made when operating the jigsaw is to start with the blade touching the workpiece; this will create a nasty kickback and unnerve the operator. First, check that the jigsaw's blade is away from the wood, cord, and any other obstructions. Next, be sure that the jigsaw's base is flat on the workpiece but the blade doesn't touch it. Then start the machine and start cutting. If the jigsaw is struggling to cut the material, check the saw settings and the blade you are using, ensuring you switch the power off at the source before you make any adjustments.

ABOVE *Your choice of finish may be dictated by many factors, such as whether your project is going to remain inside or be exposed to the elements in your yard and what your project may need to visually complement. You may find that the existing finish of the reclaimed wood can remain as it is in its new life.*

FINISH

After all of your hard work creating beautiful furniture, it's easy to fall into the trap of feeling it is time to relax when it comes to finishing a project. However, a poorly applied finish can ruin a piece of work, sometimes irreparably.

A good finish starts with the sanding process. If you are applying a clear finish, make sure all sanding is carried out working with the direction of the wood grain; this avoids cross-grain scratches that will show under the finish, ruining the effect. If you are not using an electric sander, wrap the sandpaper around a block of wood or, better still, a cork sanding block, which will help keep the sanding strokes even on flat surfaces.

Before you apply any finish to your projects, first read the manufacturer's instructions, then do a test sample, so that you know how the finish looks and how best to apply it.

Finally, as with all woodworking techniques and equipment, work safely. Wear a good-quality dust mask when you are sanding, and if you are applying a finish, wear gloves and eye protection and work in a well-ventilated area or outdoors.

BARN-STYLE DOGHOUSE

Based on the classic red barn, complete
with trim, this simple project will make
a cozy outdoor house for your dog. The
doghouse is built around a wood pallet,
something that can be picked up from a
construction site or industrial building.

I've painted this doghouse in the
familiar colors of countless barns across
the country; however, the project looks
great in a range of colors, especially
if you're making two or three. Before
purchasing the paints, check to verify
that they are suitable for exterior use
and, more important, safe for animals.

Tape measure and pencil

Claw hammer

Flat-head screwdriver

Clamp

Handsaw

Sandpaper, 50-grit,
and woodblock

Hand drill with ¼-in/6-mm
and ⅜-in/10-mm drill bits

FOR AN EASY LIFE

Jigsaw

Cordless drill/driver

EXTRAS

Wood screws

Nails

LUMBER CUTTING LIST

One pallet (for the base)

¼-in/6-mm hardboard or
other manufactured board
(for the floor)

Two ¾-by-19-by-22-in/
2-by-48-by-56-cm plywood
sheets (for the front and
back sections)

Eight ½-by-1-by-12-in/
1-by-2.5-by-31-cm boards
(for corner and door trims)

Two ¾-by-16-by-28-in/
2-by-40-by-71-cm plywood
sheets (for the side sections)

Four 12-in 2×2/
5-by-5-by-31-cm boards
(for the battens)

Ten ¾-by-4½-by-30½-in/
2-by-11.5-by-77-cm planks
(for the roof)

CHOOSING YOUR MATERIALS

Ideally, you'll need a pallet that's not too heavy, but more important—because the size of the dog barn is based on the size of the pallet—it needs to be the right size for your pet. If it's too large, your dog won't feel comfortable and it could be drafty, but if it's too small, your dog can become overheated. There are various formulas for deciding the size of a doghouse, with the most basic one being that it should be big enough for your dog to be able to turn around in comfortably, yet still be small enough to keep the dimensions of the house cozy. Most standard pallets will be suitable for only the largest of dogs, so you'll probably need to cut the pallet down to size to make it a suitable base.

You'll need to measure your dog to determine the size of the doghouse. As a general rule of thumb: for the depth of the dog barn, add 12 in/ 31 cm to your dog's length; for the width of the barn, add 18 in/46 cm to the length of the dog; and for the height of the barn, add 2 in/5 cm to your dog's sitting height, plus the height of the pallet being used as the base. Make the height of the door a little less than the height of your dog's shoulder—dogs don't mind ducking down to get into the space, and it will make your pooch feel more comfortable once inside.

From the site where I found my pallet, I also picked up a discarded 4×8/ 1.2-by-2.4-m sheet of exterior-grade ¾-in-/2-cm-thick plywood. A lot of different types of manufactured wood are used on construction sites, and with some hunting, you can find great stuff on its way to the Dumpster. The plywood was used for the front, end, and side sections of the barn. You'll also need a thin sheet of manufactured wood to cover the pallet. Some old, but sound, rescued fence planks were perfect for making the barn roof. One word of warning: if you don't know what wood preservatives have been used on reclaimed wood, don't use it for the doghouse—arsenic was used in some older preservatives.

Steps

1 If the size of the pallet is fine, move on to step 3. If you need to reduce the size of the pallet, using the tape measure and pencil, measure and mark the depth and width you'll need for the dog barn, starting from one corner so that you'll need to cut only two sides. Adjust the measurements so that the end pieces will be cut flush with the last remaining horizontal slat on the side being cut.

2 Using the claw hammer and flat-head screwdriver, pry off the piece of the pallet that supports the end that is being trimmed down. Cut along the pencil marks on the two sides with the handsaw, and trim down the end piece to fit. Reattach the end piece to the pallet, using long wood screws going through the top and at least halfway into the end piece.

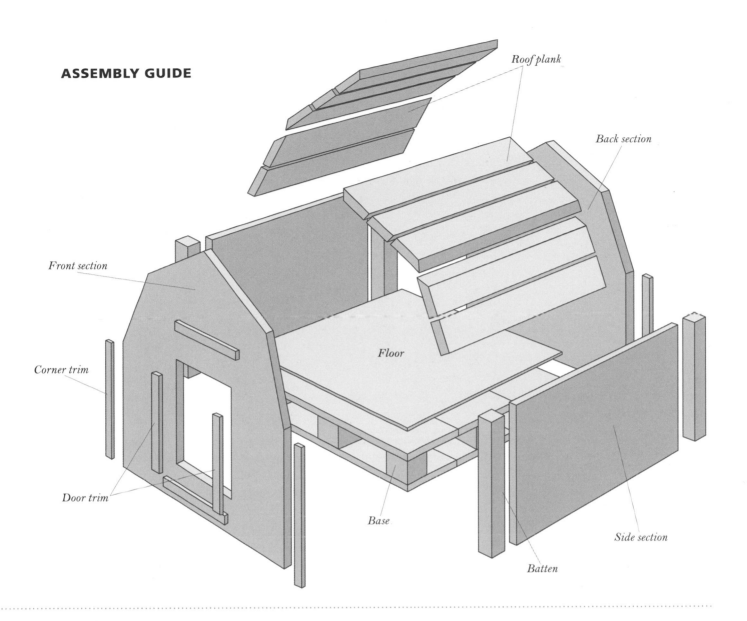

Roof plank

Back section

Front section

Corner trim

Door trim

Floor

Base

Batten

Side section

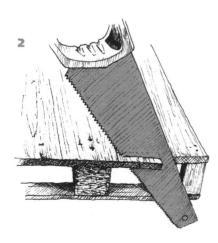

2

3 Give your pallet a quick rubdown with the 50-grit sandpaper to remove any nasty splinters, which are unpleasant for humans and animals alike. Measure and mark out the depth and width of the pallet onto a ¼-in-/6-mm-thick piece of hardboard for the floor. Cut along the pencil marks with the handsaw, then secure it to the top of the pallet with wood screws. It will make the dog barn more comfortable for your dog and help when it comes to cleaning it out.

Continued

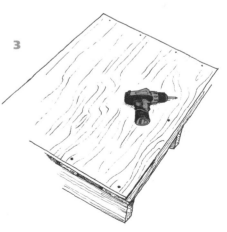

3

TIPS

- **STEP 5** A jigsaw will be easier than a handsaw and you won't need to drill as many holes.

Always be aware of where your fingers are when using either a handsaw or jigsaw.

If possible, get someone to help steady the plywood while you are cutting.

When you are cutting manufactured wood, always wear a good-quality dust mask.

4 For the front section of the barn, mark out on the bottom edge of the sheet of plywood the width of the narrow end of your pallet, then add twice the thickness of the sheet for the side sections (so the front overlaps them). Draw a vertical line up the center of the sheet, then measure up from the bottom along the centerline and mark the height of the barn based on your dog's size (see Choosing Your Materials, page 22). From this point to each side, mark and draw an attractive barn roof shape, then mark out the sides back down to the edges of the base.

5 Next, measure and mark out the square hole for the door. Make it to a size that suits your dog (see Choosing Your Materials, page 22), but mark the bottom of the door so it will be flush with the hardboard on top of the pallet. Clamp the board in place, then using the handsaw, cut around the shape of the front section. To cut out the door opening, start by drilling a line of overlapping ⅜-in/10-mm holes near a pencil line on each side of the opening until you can fit the saw blade in, then cut the opening with a handsaw.

6 For the back section of the barn, place the front section on the plywood sheet and use the pencil to draw around it, then cut along the pencil marks with the handsaw.

7 For the trim, measure, cut, and glue and nail ½-by-1-in/1-by-2.5-cm boards around the door and at the two side edges of the front and back sections. Make angled cuts for near the roof.

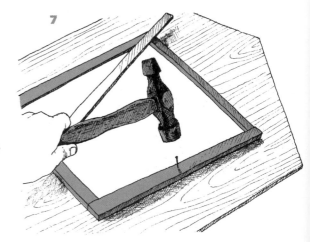

8 Measure and cut two side sections to the same length of the pallet's long edge and the same height of the front section at the lowest point of the roof. Mark a horizontal line at the bottom of each end the height of the pallet. Using the handsaw, cut four 12-in 2×2/5-by-5-by-31-cm wood battens, and drill two ¼-in/6-mm pilot holes in each of two adjacent faces, keeping them staggered. Using wood screws, attach a batten above the pencil mark on each end of the two side sections.

9 Now it's time to start assembling the dog barn. Position the front section and one of the side sections lined up with the pallet, then secure them together by driving a screw into each batten. Continue with the next side section and the back section until all four sections are joined together.

10 For the roof, cut the planks the length of the side sections with an extra 2 in/5 cm to overhang the front and back. The two planks that butt together at the peak of the roof need to be cut down one length at an angle. Put one piece in position on the roof and draw a vertical line up, then repeat with the second piece. If you don't have a table saw, ask a local carpenter to cut down the length of the planks at this angle. Nail the top two roof planks in place, then line up each following plank and nail in place, one at a time.

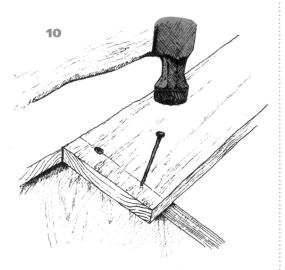

TIPS

- **STEP 10** Depending on the angles you've created for the roof, you will probably have to make angled cuts where the roof slope changes direction—position the bottom planks first and measure and cut in a similar way as for the peak, but mark the cut to align with the top slope of the roof, then position the remaining planks and, if necessary, cut the final plank at an angle as well.

To help align the nails over the top edges of the barn sides below, measure and draw a pencil line to follow.

If you live in an area where it would be prudent to have extra weatherproofing, nail a scrap of roofing felt to the roof.

If you live in an area with cold winters, you can add insulation to the dog barn. You'll need to make double layers of the floor and walls to sandwich the insulation between them.

I chose to paint the finished doghouse. I used three colors for the classic barn effect: white for the door and corner trim, red for the walls, and slate gray for the roof.

The completed barn-style doghouse.

(A) *Weathered fence planks make attractive roofing material.* **(B)** *When fitting the trim at the corners and around the door opening, keep them flush to the edges of the other pieces.* **(C)** *The battens inside the doghouse don't need to extend all the way up the sides—just make sure there's room to fit them below the roof and above the pallet.* **(D)** *Keep the edges of the planks you've used for the roof close together to ensure the maximum protection from the weather for your pet.* **(E)** *The roof planks where the two halves meet at the top have been cut at an angle for a snugger fit and to keep out the elements.*

RUSTIC HALF-LOG BENCH

I have to thank a buddy of mine for this idea. The only thing he inherited from his grandpa was an old, much-used log sawhorse that sat on his porch. It is one of those simple objects that has history written all over it. This gray-green sawhorse carried the battle scars of many years of hard labor. Now in a well-earned retirement, it proudly stands cradling its last half log, with its only task to display a few old flowerpots. I liked it so much that I decided I had to make one of my own. I intended to use my bench to display stuff instead of to sit on, so I made it on the high side. However, you can make it to a height that suits your needs. Okay, mine may not have the same history at the moment, but who knows...by the time my grandkids get it, it may.

TOOLS FOR THE JOB

Tape measure and pencil

Hand drill with ³⁄₁₆-in/4-mm
drill bit

Handsaw

Surform plane or
wood rasp

Clamps

Sandpaper, 80- and
120-grit, and woodblock

FOR AN EASY LIFE

Electric sander

EXTRAS

Wood screws

Varnish of your choice

LUMBER CUTTING LIST

Four 2-by-3-by-30 in/
5-by-7.5-by-76-cm boards
(for the X legs)

Two 32-in 1×4/2.5-by-10-
by-82-cm boards (for the
cross rails)

One 36-in/91-cm half log
(for the bench top)

CHOOSING YOUR MATERIALS

It will help if you have the half log for the top before you get started because it will give you the proportions needed for the X frame. For my bench, I had an old split fence post 36 in/91 cm long and 9 in/23 cm wide. However, you can also use a split log if you are handy with an axe. In this case, a cedar log is a good choice if you want your bench to last in the outdoor elements.

I chose for my X legs some rough sawn pieces of 2-by-3-in/5-by-7.5-cm lumber, which I hoped would give my bench an aged feel. Because of the weight the frame will have to take when supporting the log, make sure you use sound, thick lumber. A nice detail for the top of the X legs is to shape them. You could opt for straightforward rounded ends or, as I did, you could make them into an arched shape.

The only other component in this simple project are the two cross rails in the frame. I chose two 1×4/2.5-by-10-cm boards that were 32 in/82 cm long. They will establish the distance between the X legs, so make sure they are long enough to make the frame sturdy enough to support the log. I've made mine just slightly shorter than the log, but you can make yours the same length of the log or even a little longer.

You may want to stick to the homespun rustic look and keep your half log in the same rough-hewn state you found it. Or maybe, like me, you prefer the contrast of a rough frame and a smooth log top. If you've chosen the latter path, then I'm afraid that look doesn't come cheap, and the price is a lot of muscle work. If you are using a log from the woods, you'll need to do even more work to remove the bark—either peeling it off, using a chisel and mallet to pry it off, or using a drawknife—but better still, simply leave the bark on.

TIP

- **STEP 2** You can use nails instead of wood screws, but screws have a pulling effect, making the finished joint a little stronger.

Steps

❶ Lay out the wood for two of the legs into an X shape, and measure between them the width of the half log to be held. With this worked out, mark the angles of the joint where the pieces meet, using the pencil.

ASSEMBLY GUIDE

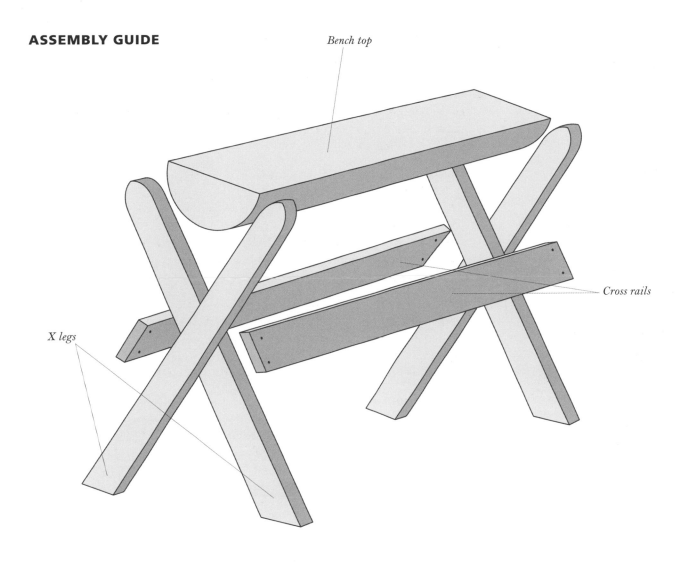

Bench top

X legs

Cross rails

2 With the joint lines marked on the legs, drill two pilot holes with the ³⁄₁₆-in/4-mm drill bit, one above the other, on just one of the two legs of the X frame. Position the legs together again, and fasten them with long wood screws. Repeat this process on the second pair of X legs.

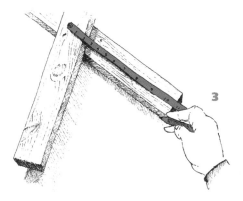

3 You now need to cut an angle at the bottom of the leg so that it will sit squarely on the floor. Using the tape measure, mark with the pencil on the inside of the leg the height you want your bench to be, making sure the marks are an equal distance from the center of the X joint. My bench was 21 in/53 cm high.

Continued

TIP

• **STEP 5** When you have finished with the template, store it for future use instead of discarding it. You never know when an opportunity to make a second project may arise.

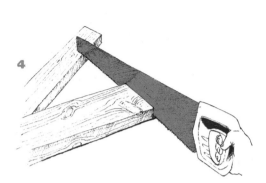

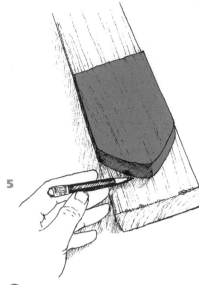

4 Lay a wood strip or ruler onto the legs, connecting the pencil marks to create flat, even ends, and draw a line across both, then cut across the line with the handsaw.

5 Whichever shape you choose for the top of the legs, the process for shaping them is the same. Using a scrap piece of cardboard, paper, or wood of the same width of the leg, first draw, then cut out your shape. Transfer this template onto each of the top ends of the X leg frames. Using the handsaw, cut off the corners, and then, using the Surform plane or wood rasp, smooth down the shape to the pencil line.

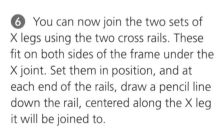

6 You can now join the two sets of X legs using the two cross rails. These fit on both sides of the frame under the X joint. Set them in position, and at each end of the rails, draw a pencil line down the rail, centered along the X leg it will be joined to.

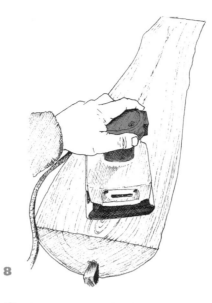

7 Using the ³⁄₁₆-in/4-mm drill bit, drill two pilot holes along each pencil line. Next attach the rails to the legs using wood screws. You should now have a sawhorse ready for a log.

8 If your log is as rough as mine, it will need a lot of attention from the Surform plane and sander if you want a smooth finish. Start by clamping the log to a bench. Using the coarse Surform plane, smooth down the log to get a reasonably flat surface, then change to 80-grit sandpaper; if you can attach it to an electric sander, the task ahead shouldn't be too bad. If, however, you are just running on muscle power, you are about to get a great workout. Change to 120-grit sandpaper when you feel the top is getting close to a decent finish.

9 Position the sanded half log in the frame, and with the ³⁄₁₆-in/4-mm drill bit, drill pilot holes in the underside of the top of the legs, angling the drill so that the holes will connect with the log. Insert wood screws into the holes and secure them in place. Make sure the screws are long enough to go through the legs and securely into the log.

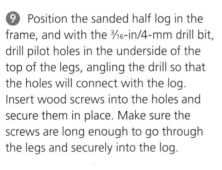

TIPS

- **STEP 8** If you don't have clamps, nail four sturdy cleats to the bench with the log wedged firmly in the middle.

You will find working with the grain avoids cross-grain scratches, which will impair the quality of any clear finish applied. As the grit on the sandpaper gets finer, make sure you sand in the direction of the grain, not against it.

However you sand the wood, always wear a good-quality dust mask.

- **STEP 9** Rubbing wood screws against an old wax candle will make it easier to drive them into the wood.

If you've put a lot of work into sanding the log, you'll want a finish that brings out all of its natural beauty. My choice would be one of the wood oils on the market. It won't be as robust in all-weather conditions as some exterior finishes, but an oil finish makes up for this in the way it enriches and highlights the grain pattern. Alternatively, coat the rough framework in an exterior wood stain, and the top in a satin sheen exterior varnish.

The completed rustic half-log bench.

(A) The rings on the ends of the half log are an attractive feature that should be kept exposed. **(B)** This is a simple frame to assemble, with just a few pieces involved, but it is also sturdy. **(C)** All the work you put into sanding the top to a smooth finish will be appreciated when you see the finished result. **(D)** I chose to keep the frame a natural color, which works with the log, but you could paint the frame instead. **(E)** The bottom of the log used for the bench top can be left in its original state.

AXE-HANDLE
TABLE

At least 80 percent of the hand tools in my workshop have been picked up in either a yard sale or flea market. Not only are they vastly cheaper than buying new ones, but in most cases I think they are better made. I was at a yard sale, taking a look at a hatchet from a box of old tools, when I caught sight of a small reproduction table with striking French-style cabriole legs. Looking from the curve of these legs back to the similar curve of my hatchet handle, I had the idea for this table.

TOOLS FOR THE JOB

Flat-head screwdriver

Sandpaper, 80- and
120-grit, and woodblock

Pencil

Workbench or a pair of
sawhorses

Scrap wood

Hand drill with ½-in/
12-mm drill bit

Handsaw

Claw hammer

FOR AN EASY LIFE

Electric sander

EXTRAS

Wood glue

Linseed oil

LUMBER CUTTING LIST

One 2-by-12-by-31½-in/
5-by-31-by-80-cm plank
(for the tabletop)

Four 13-in/33-cm-long
axe handles (for the legs)

Scrap wood (to make four
wedges for the leg joints)

TIP

• **STEP 2** No matter how you
sand the top—by hand or
machine—always wear a
dust mask.

CHOOSING YOUR MATERIALS

The essential components in this project are, of course, the four axe handles to make the legs—you will need four handles of the same size. Because axe handles come in just a few standard sizes, such as 13 in/ 33 cm, 16 in/40 cm, and so on, finding a matching set shouldn't be too difficult. You probably won't find four handles that will match exactly in curve and color; however, don't worry about this—it's part of the idiosyncratic charm of this project. The legs of the table will look best if set splayed out at about a 45-degree angle.

The length of the handles will dictate the size of tabletop you will need. Lay two handles on the floor and move them apart until you have a width and length that looks right to you. This will be the rough proportion of the top you will be looking for. Whatever the dimensions of your chosen piece of wood, you will need something that has a decent thickness, at least 2 in/5 cm, to make good, deep joints to produce a sturdy table.

You may already have set aside an attractive piece of solid wood, saving it for a special project to give it a chance to shine; this will be the perfect opportunity to use it. If not, a good place to start your search is the local lumberyard. The table needs a top with a lot of life and wild grain patterns. For this, you should look for lumber taken from either the "crotch" of the tree—this is the point where the main branches start to flare away from the trunk—or from the bottom of the tree trunk, just where it was cut for felling.

Using an eye-catching piece of wood demands choosing a good finish to both protect the wood and enhance the grain patterns. Linseed oil is a natural finish that is perfect for the job, but you can use any clear finish.

Steps

1 Using the flat-head screwdriver, remove any loose bark from the edges of the board. Don't worry if you find splits in the ends of the wood; as long as they don't run close to the length of the whole board, or travel close to a leg position, they won't affect the table's strength.

2 Using the sheet of 80-grit sandpaper wrapped around a woodblock, sand the face of the board you think will look best as the top of the table. (This is a tough job; using an electric sander will avoid a lot of muscle ache later on.)

ASSEMBLY GUIDE

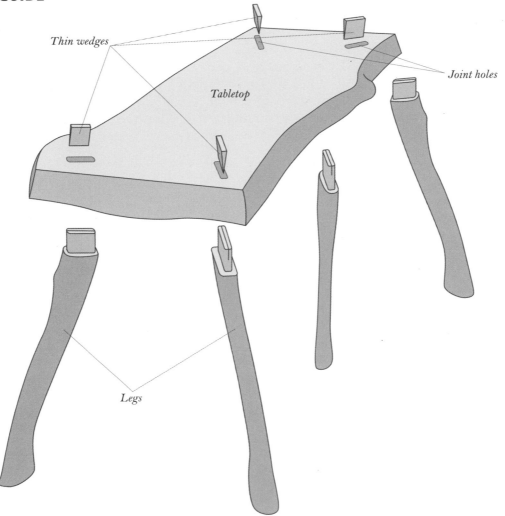

Thin wedges

Joint holes

Tabletop

Legs

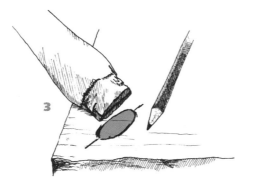

3 The next few steps can determine the table's success, so take your time. Mark the positions for the legs onto the sanded face of the tabletop, tracing around the legs with the pencil. Accuracy is not critical, as long as they look in line by eye. These mark where to drill out the holes for the leg joints.

Continued

TIP

• STEP 3 The eye can be a great tool when making things. However, it has to be trained to perform tasks, such as checking if a line is true, a curve smooth, or, as in this case, the legs are in line. Once you have it trained, trust it.

TIPS

- Leftover axe heads can have many different uses; hammered into wooden fence posts, they make attractive points to attach garden twine for climbing plants, and they are handy used as doorstops around the house.

- When knocking off the axe heads with a hammer, always wear eye protection and be careful of your toes.

- After felling and planking, lumber is stacked to dry, sometimes for years. The ends of the planks lose moisture more quickly than the rest of the wood, and as a result they are prone to movement and splitting. For this reason, lumberyards will discard these sections, or at least sell them for lower prices.

- STEP 6 Place a piece of scrap wood underneath the piece you are drilling; this will stop the wood from splintering as the drill emerges.

Always wear safety goggles when using a drill.

If you are unsure about making the angled holes for the joint, practice drilling them on a piece of scrap wood before working on the tabletop.

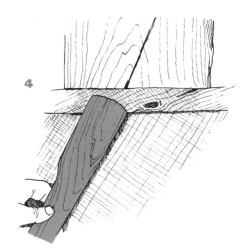

4 The only way to set the legs splayed out is to make the joint holes at an angle. Make a guide for the drill: rest the tabletop on the workbench with one end overhanging the edge. Put a scrap of wood on end on the tabletop. Hold a leg below the tabletop at a 45-degree angle. With the pencil, continue the angle up across the scrap wood. If someone is nearby to lend a hand, this is a good time to enlist help.

6 Carefully drill out the shape of the joint, making overlapping holes. Repeat steps 5 and 6 for each of the four legs.

5 Position the marked scrap wood where you want to make an angled joint hole, making sure the angle is going in the correct direction. Using the ½-in/12-mm drill bit (or one that matches the handle's diameter), set the drill on the tabletop, lining it up by eye against the angle on the scrap wood.

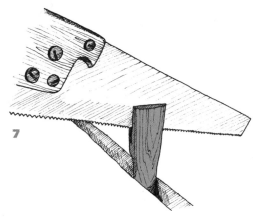

7 Adding a wedge in the joint will add extra strength. Using the handsaw, cut a slot into the joint end of the axe handles as deep as the thickness of the tabletop. Again using the handsaw, cut four thin wedges shorter than the cut in the axe handle and about ¼ in/6 mm at the thick end of the wedges.

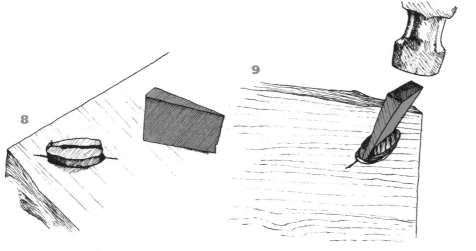

8 Flip the tabletop onto its face so the underside faces up, then add a good amount of wood glue to each hole, and force in each leg until slightly protruding from the top of the table. Turning the table up onto its new legs, check by eye that the legs are sitting correctly, and adjust them as necessary until you are happy with the positioning of all four legs.

9 Use a claw hammer to tap the wedges into the slots made in the leg ends. Start gently but finish with a couple of good blows. Let the glue dry overnight.

TIPS

- **STEP 8** If the table wobbles, set it on a flat surface and find the leg that is too long. Trim a small amount off with a saw until it sits evenly without wobbling.

- **STEP 10** I chose an oil-base finish (linseed oil) for my table. Although it is not as durable as some exterior finishes, it will show off the natural beauty of the wood. Apply at least three coats, sanding down with 120-grit sandpaper between each application.

If you are using a cloth to apply an oil finish, be especially careful when disposing of it after use. Rolled or scrunched up oil-soaked cloths are a potential fire hazard and have been known to spontaneously combust.

10 When you return to your project the next day, trim away the protruding part of the axe handles and wedges with the handsaw. Next, sand each one flush using 80-grit sandpaper, then use 120-grit sandpaper until they are smooth.

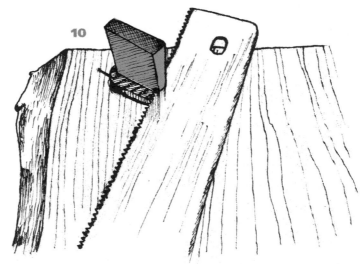

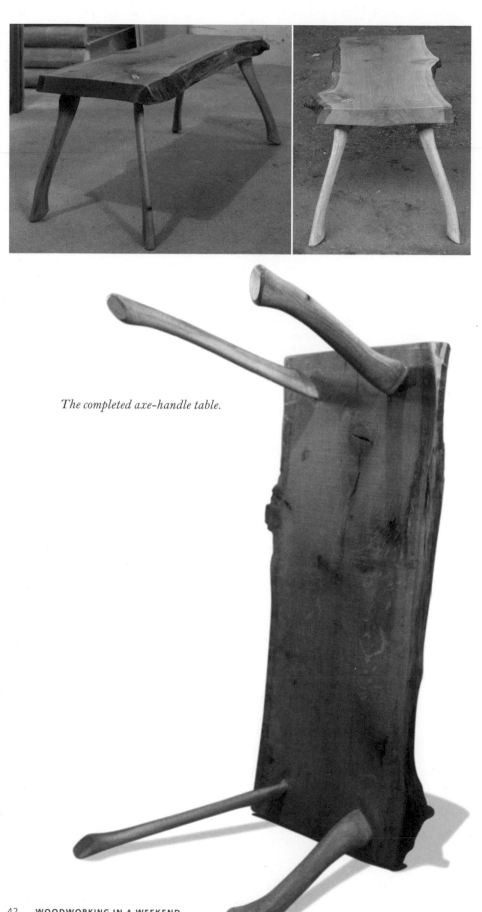

The completed axe-handle table.

(A) *Trimmed-off branch stubs create an interesting feature.* **(B)** *The relatively straight grain of the top contrasts with the rough texture of the bark along the edge.* **(C)** *Wavy grain along the smooth surface of the rough-hewn wood makes this an eye-catching tabletop.* **(D)** *The curve near where the blade was once held in the handle adds an interesting shape to the legs.*

LADDER PLANT STAND

I had a wooden ladder that had seen better days—what few rungs it still had were too rotten to stand on. Instead of throwing it out, along with three old scaffolding planks, it could be transformed into a stand onto which planters with cascading and climbing plants will thrive. Trying to buy something similar in a store can be expensive, yet it's easy to build yourself. Besides—you will also have the pleasure of making your own unique planter stand. It has to be a worth a few hours spent in the workshop or garage.

TOOLS FOR THE JOB

Tape measure and pencil

Handsaw

Wood rasp

Screwdriver or claw hammer

Clamps

Hand drill with ⅜-in/ 10-mm and ³⁄₁₆-in/4-mm drill bits

FOR AN EASY LIFE

Cordless drill/driver

EXTRAS

Wood screws or nails

LUMBER CUTTING LIST

One wooden ladder

One 1¼-by-9-by-39-in/ 3-by-23-by-99-cm board (for the top shelf)

One 1¼-by-9-by-52-in/ 3-by-23-by-132-cm board (for the middle shelf)

One 1¼-by-9-by-62½-in/ 3-by-23-by-159-cm board (for the bottom shelf)

One 6-ft 1×2/2.5-by-5-by- 180-cm board (for the shelf supports)

CHOOSING YOUR MATERIALS

The ladder I chose for this project was missing a few rungs as a result of many years of hard work. One had broken away just at a point where I intended to place a shelf support, but to not fit a shelf at this point would make my rack too small. You can substitute another rung that won't be needed, or purchase dowel from a home-improvement center that has the same diameter as your rung. The wood won't look the same, so consider an opaque paint finish.

Old scaffolding planks are the perfect choice for the shelves. They are made from good-quality 1¼-in-/3-cm-thick lumber that is suitable for outdoor use. Any solid lumber boards of a similar thickness will do as an alternative. You'll also need 1×2/2.5-by-5-cm boards for shelf supports.

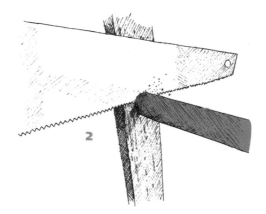

Steps

1 Decide on the height you want your plant stand to be, which might be decided by the quality of the ladder you have to use. You'll need two equal sections of the ladder, so take that into consideration when deciding the final height. Using a tape measure and pencil, measure and mark where the ladder will need to be cut in half, then cut it in half with the handsaw. If you don't need to replace a rung, move on to step 3; to replace a rung to support a shelf, follow step 2.

2 To replace a rung, borrow one from another part of the ladder where you don't want to attach a shelf. Cut one end of the chosen rung with the handsaw, making the cut close to the ladder's side rail, then wiggle the rung so that it comes out. Smooth the cut end with a wood rasp, then slip the rung into the two holes left in the ladder's side rails by the missing rung. If you don't have a snug fit, secure the rung in place by driving a screw through each side rail into the ends of the rung.

Continued

ASSEMBLY GUIDE

Ladder

Top shelf

Middle shelf

Bottom shelf

Shelf supports

- **STEP 3** I like the look of the top ends extending above the top shelf, but you can shorten them if you feel they will be in the way when watering the plants.

- **STEP 4** An extra pair of hands can be helpful for either steadying the ladders or holding the tape measure.

- **STEP 5** To make sure all the corners are the same, after cutting off the first corner, use the scrap corner piece as a template to measure and mark the remaining corners.

3 Line up the two side rails side by side. Check that the rungs are parallel with each other. If they are not, measure, mark, and cut the ladder ends, with the handsaw, until they match. At this point, the ends of the four side rails should all be cut at equal right angles (the ends will be shaped later on to sit level on the ground).

4 Position the two equal ladder sections on their edges in an A shape that you find pleasing to the eye: not so tight that the effect of the diagonals is lost, but not so wide that the ladder sections look as though they will do the splits. With a tape measure and pencil, mark the distance between the opposing rungs where you want shelves, with a minimum of two—one at the top and one at the bottom—and make a note of the measurements.

5 For each shelf, add 12 in/31 cm to the measurement so the shelf has a 6-in/15-cm overhang on each end, measure and mark the board and, using the handsaw, cut the board to length. To add some detail and prevent injuries, cut off the corners.

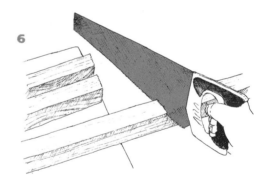

6 To make supports for each shelf, using the handsaw, cut four lengths of 1×2/2.5-by-5-cm board that are ½ in/1 cm shorter than the width of the shelf. Repeat for each shelf, so you have four supports per shelf.

7

8

7 Clamp a shelf support, with the thin edge facing up, to a scrap board and drill two ⅜-in/10-mm holes one-quarter of the way into the side edge, about 1 in/2.5 cm from the end. Now, fit a ³⁄₁₆-in/4-mm bit in the drill and continue the hole right through. (This will allow you to fit a slightly shorter screw into the edge so all the screws used in the project will be the same size.) Repeat for each shelf support.

8 Working one at a time, reposition each shelf support so the wide side is facedown, clamp in place, and drill one ³⁄₁₆-in/4-mm hole in the center of the block.

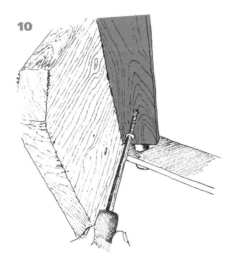

10

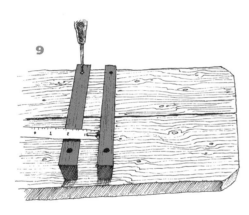

9

9 Measure in 6 in/15 cm from the end of the shelf and attach one of the shelf supports, driving screws through the face with two holes. Measure the ladder rung's thickness from the inside edge of the secured support toward the shelf's center, then secure a second support here. Repeat on the other end of the shelf, then repeat on all the shelves.

10 With the ladder sections resting on their sides, fit all the shelves in place. If everything looks okay, start driving in the screws. Drive in one screw through the shelf support into the rung. Drive at least two screws through each shelf's top into the rung.

11 With the stand upright, lay a ¾-in/2-cm woodblock against the bottom of the ladder. Draw a pencil mark along the top of the block onto the end of the stand's legs. Trim the legs with the handsaw along these marks so the feet sit flush with the floor. Finally, round off the ladder tops with a rasp. The ladder plant stand is finished and ready for decoration and flowerpots.

TIPS

- **STEP 7** If you don't have a depth guide for your drill, wrap a piece of masking tape around the drill bit at the desired depth to act as a guide when you are making the first hole one-quarter of the way into the edge.

- **STEP 10** You can use nails instead of screws if you prefer, but screws provide a stronger joint than nails, and are easier if you want to disassemble the project.

- **STEP 11** For a little more originality, you can make plant boxes. Using some odd lengths of decking, I made several boxes from different lengths to fit the shelf length. Most wood decking has been pretreated for weather. Work out the quantity and sizes of boxes you require. Cut the parts to size with a handsaw, and simply nail together.

The completed
ladder plant stand.

(A) *Simply trimming off the corners on the shelves will mean less accidents.* **(B)** *The sides of the plant boxes are simply butted together—no fancy joints necessary.* **(C)** *The wood supports attached to the bottom of the shelves slip over the rungs on the ladders, helping to hold everything together.* **(D)** *It's not necessary to round off the top of the ladders, but I prefer the look.* **(E)** *The screws will provide a longer-lasting stand than if assembled with nails.*

THREE-DOOR SCREEN

Despite all of our best intentions, many yards have areas that are just a little unsightly. It could be where the garbage cans are kept, the pile of kids' outdoor toys, barbecue equipment, or just the place where the yard clutter finds its home. If you have something to hide, why not try making this three-door screen? Even if you have a clutter-free yard, the screen will make a striking feature. You can use it to create a more private secluded area or for creating shade from the sun and shelter from a breeze.

TOOLS FOR THE JOB

Jigsaw or handsaw

Tape measure and pencil

Hand drill with ³⁄₁₆-in/4-mm drill bit

Screwdriver

FOR AN EASY LIFE

Cordless drill/driver

EXTRAS

Wood screws

Four 3-in/7.5-cm butt hinges

CUTTING LIST

Three 30-by-78-in/ 76-by-198-cm doors

Two 1-by-6-by-12-in/ 2.5-by-15-by-31-cm boards (for the feet)

CHOOSING YOUR MATERIALS

This is a project that is open to your own creative interpretation. Although simple to build, the screen can be painted, sanded down to its natural wood or, as I have done, made with a combination of the two.

You'll need to find three doors. The doors don't need to match, and sometimes it can look better if they don't. I picked up mine from a house that was being refurbished. The doors had been left on a pile of old lumber ready to be burned; after a polite inquiry, the site foreman was only too happy for me to take them away, along with some of the other lumber. Another place to check is your local junkyard; it can be a great source for all types of material.

If you want the natural wood look but the doors have already been painted, there are two options open to you: either bring them to a commercial paint stripping company to have them professionally stripped, or do it yourself, using a chemical stripping compound from the hardware store or—my preferred method—a heat gun. You can pick up a heat gun at a reasonable price these days, and the initial investment will be paid back with all the other stripping projects that crop up around the home. After stripping the paint away, sand the door with 120-grit sandpaper wrapped around a block of wood, or an electric sander.

Hopefully, your old doors should come with their original hinges; however, if they don't, go to the local hardware store and ask for four of their cheapest 3-in/7.5-cm butt hinges.

ASSEMBLY GUIDE

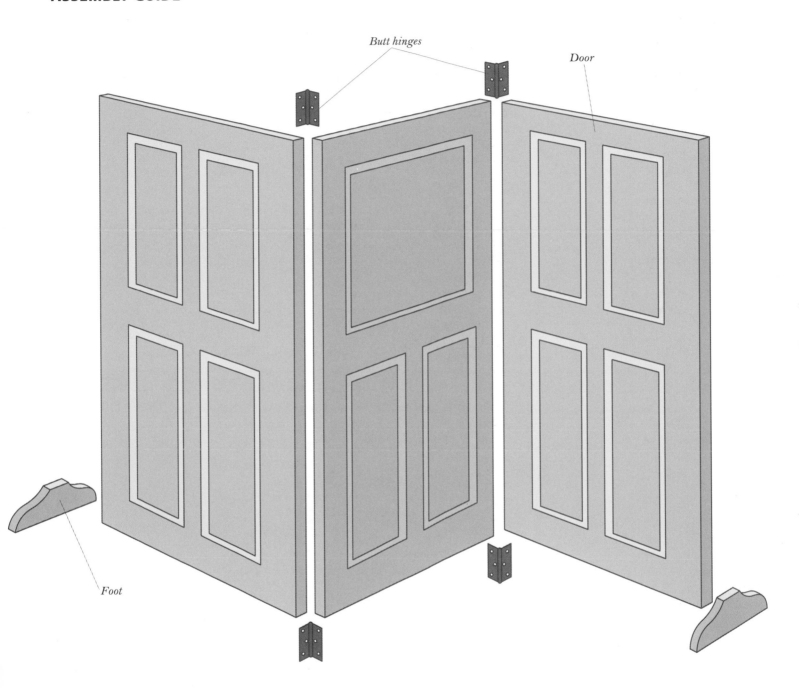

Butt hinges

Door

Foot

TIPS

- If you are using a chemical stripper to remove the paint on the doors before you start on the project, wear protective gloves and safety goggles. Always follow the manufacturer's instructions.

- **STEP 2** If you have a jigsaw, you can add an attractive curve to the feet; if you don't, try cutting an angle off each top corner with a handsaw to help lighten the appearance.

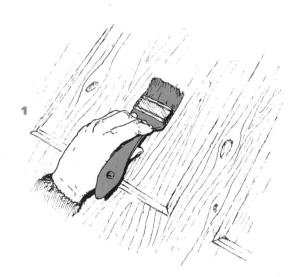

Steps

1 If you want to paint or varnish your doors, it is best to do so now, before assembling them. If you prefer their natural wood finish, apply a few coats of a clear exterior varnish to provide some protection from the weather. If you want to change the color, apply one or two coats of exterior paint.

2 The screen will need some way of adding stability to keep it standing on gusty days. Cut two support feet from wood that has a thickness of at least 1 in/2.5 cm, and is about 12 in/31 cm long and 6 in/15 cm high.

3 On each support foot, draw a pencil line down the center, then drill three evenly spaced holes with the ³⁄₁₆-in/4-mm drill bit.

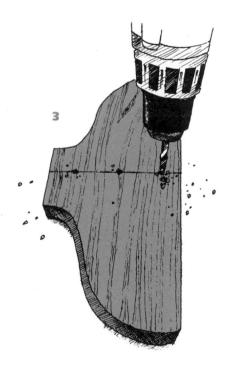

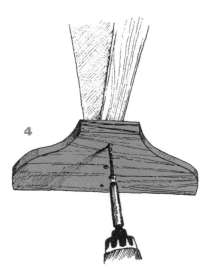

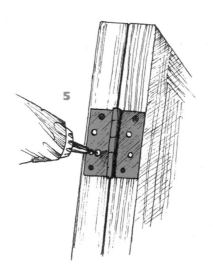

- **STEP 4** Having an extra pair of hands will help when steadying the doors to work on.

- **STEP 5** When fitting the butt joint in place, make sure the middle part of the hinge will be clear of the door's edge. This will create a gap where the doors meet; without such a gap the doors will rub or bind together.

④ Line up one foot so it is flush with the bottom of the first door's edge and secure it into position with wood screws; the screws should be long enough to go about 2 in/5 cm into the door. Attach the other foot at the bottom edge of the third door in the same way.

⑤ Lay the doors against a wall in the correct sequence. Starting with the first door, screw the hinges in place about 4 in/10 cm from the top and bottom of the edge of the door without a foot. Do the same with the last door, only this time make sure the butt joint of the hinges is facing the opposite way from the ones on the first door. Now, with some buddy help, screw these two outer doors to the middle door. Keeping the doors flat against each other will help when doing this.

OPTIONAL STEP

If one of the doors has an empty hole where there would have been glass, fill it with a panel of manufactured board. Paint the panel with exterior paint or blackboard paint, which is handy for leaving notes to your loved ones, drawing garden plans, or just writing lines from a favorite poem.

(A) *You can replace a glass panel with a manufactued board painted with blackboard paint.* **(B)** *It's not necessary for all the doors to match, nor the finishes.* **(C)** *Keep the screws straight as they go through the foot and into the edge of the door.* **(D)** *Make sure the flaps of the screw hinges are not wider than the edge of the doors.*

The completed three-door screen.

A

B

D

C

BREEZY TABLE

This project is quick and easy. It doesn't require a lot of lumber, it's fun to make, and the end result is an attractive little table with a number of different uses. Paint it or leave it natural—either works well. I've even made a few out of old advertising boards, the graphics of which made them real statement pieces. My kids have one with a top I painted in blackboard paint from the hardware store—it's one piece of furniture I'm happy for them to draw on.

TOOLS FOR THE JOB

Hand drill with ¼-in/6-mm
and ³⁄₁₆-in/4-mm drill bits

Tape measure and 2 pencils

Claw hammer

Clamps

Jigsaw

Wood rasp or
Surform plane

Sandpaper, 80- and
120-grit, and woodblock

Straightedge or length
of straight board

Triangle

Flat-head screwdriver

Handsaw

Vise

FOR AN EASY LIFE

Cordless drill/driver

Electric sander

EXTRAS

Nails

Wood glue

Wood screws

LUMBER CUTTING LIST

One ½-by-1-by-18-in/
1-by-2.5-by-46-cm board
(for the trammel)

Two ¾-by-30-by-30-in/
2-by-76-by-76-cm sheets
of manufactured wood
(for the tabletop and shelf)

Four 2½-by-3-by-18-in/
6-by-7.5-by-46-cm boards
(for the legs)

TIP

• STEP 3 When operating
the jigsaw, remember to
keep fingers and the cord
away from the blade.

CHOOSING YOUR MATERIALS

To make this table, you only need a few components: some sheet material and a few boards. Thinking about where and how you want to use the table, decide on the diameter that you want your table to be, then find either a sheet or two of manufactured wood or two solid wood panels that will be large enough to fit the diameter. The table needs two disks: one for the tabletop and one for the shelf. However, the materials you use don't need to match—in fact, using different materials can produce some interesting, creative results. For the table shown in this project, I used a scrap sheet of exterior-grade plywood.

The lumber for the legs should be something that is in proportion to your table's diameter. For example, on my table, which has a diameter of 30 in/76 cm, I used 2½-by-3-in/6-by-7.5-cm stock for the legs, which I cut to lengths of 18 in/46 cm. Each of the four legs will need two different joints. The tabletop will fit into a simple notched-out corner, known as a rabbet joint, at the top of the leg. And the shelf will fit into a slot on the leg's side—this is known as a dado joint.

To mark out the two disks, you will be using some ancient technology. The trammel, or beam compass, has been around since we discovered circles, and it's easy to make one with a long, thin board, pencil, and nail and using a drill. The exact dimensions of the board aren't important, just as long as it's wide enough to drill a hole for the pencil, longer than half the diameter of the work plus 3 in/7.5 cm to take the pencil and nail, and lightweight so it will be easy to use for scribing a circle. Likewise, if you don't have a straightedge, many woodworkers will use any length of lumber as long as it has a relatively straight edge along one side. If you like the table but don't have access to a jigsaw, you can make a square version. Cut out square boards with the handsaw and just follow the rest of the steps, except for the first steps on making the trammel.

Steps

❶ To mark the circle for the tabletop, make a trammel from a thin board that is at least 3 in/7.5 cm longer than half the diameter of your tabletop. Drill a hole into one end, using the ¼-in/6-mm drill bit, and push a pencil into the hole. Using the tape measure and the other pencil, measure and mark from the tip of the pencil half the diameter of your tabletop, then tap in a nail at this point.

❷ Tap the trammel nail into the center of the board for the tabletop and scribe a circle with the pencil end. Repeat again on the board you are using for the shelf, so you have marked two circles ready to be cut out for the table.

ASSEMBLY GUIDE

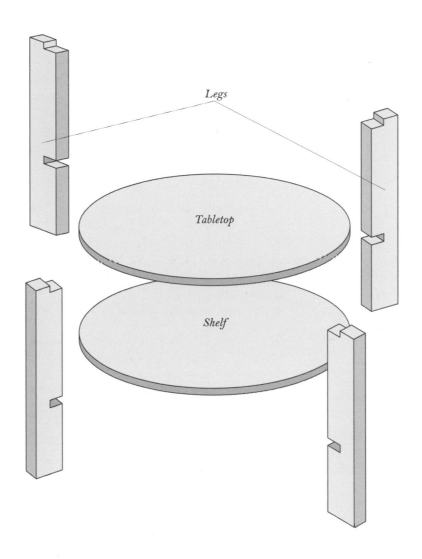

Legs

Tabletop

Shelf

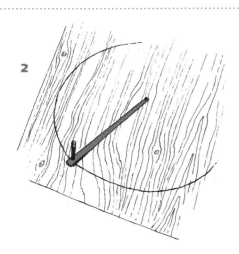

2

3 One at a time, clamp the boards safely to a stable working surface. Following the pencil lines of the scribed circles, cut out both the tabletop and the shelf with the jigsaw.

3

Continued

TIPS

- **STEP 5** There are many mathematically correct ways of working out the quarters, but a simple solution it to pick up a sheet of paper with two edges that look like they are at 90 degrees to each other (that's a right angle).

- **STEP 6** When marking right angles, curves, and circles, trust what your eye tells you. We humans have a built-in sense that tells us when something is out of line or not level. The more we trust and train this ability, the sharper it gets.

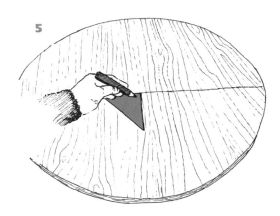

4 Stack together the two disks, aligning the edges as best you can and making sure the hole left by the trammel nail is visible on one disk, then temporarily secure the disks together by tapping in two nails. (This will help keep the disks identical as you remove any bumps left by the jigsaw.) Use a wood rasp or Surform plane to remove any bumps and smooth the edges. Finish off the edges, first with 80-grit sandpaper, then 120-grit sandpaper, until they are smooth.

5 With the disks still tacked together, line up the straightedge with the small trammel nail hole, and draw a pencil line through the center of the disk face. Now, you need a line to quarter the disk. Using the triangle (or see the Tip), lay one of the right-angle edges against the pencil line with the 90-degree corner of the triangle lined up with the trammel hole, then draw a line along this second edge of the right angle. Flip the triangle over and draw a line from the trammel hole in the opposite direction.

6 Extend the pencil line to quarter the circle to the edges of the disk. Now, transfer the quarter lines onto the two disks' edges, using the pencil, so you have four points of reference, then use them and the straightedge to quarter the face of the other disk.

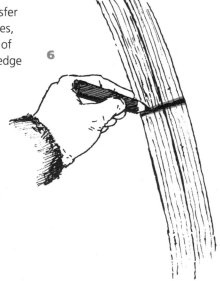

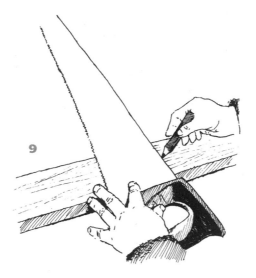

7 With both the tabletop and the shelf marked with corresponding lines, fit the flat-head screwdriver between the disks and pry them apart, then remove the nails with the claw hammer.

8 To make the legs, using the tape measure and pencil, measure and mark the length you want the legs to be on each board, then cut them with the handsaw.

9 Now, mark the positions for the joints on the legs. Make all the joints a depth just under halfway into the leg. On my 3-in-/7.5-cm-thick leg, the joints were 1¼ in/3 cm deep. For the tabletop joint, measure down from the top of the leg the same distance as the thickness of the tabletop (my top is ¾ in/2 cm deep), and draw a pencil line, then also draw the pencil line for the depth of the joint. Repeat for the other three legs.

TIPS

- **STEP 10** Measure and mark up one leg, then use it to transfer the joint lines onto the other three legs. This will ensure that all the joints are uniform—and it will reduce the amount of measuring you'll need to do.

After marking out your joints, draw pencil lines onto the waste to be removed; this will help reassure you that you're cutting in the right place when working in full flow.

10 Now measure and mark the joints for the shelf. I set the shelf on my table 4¾ in/12 cm up from the bottom end of the legs. However, you can make it whatever height works for your table. Mark the joint for the thickness of the shelf board (again, I used a ¾-in-/2-cm-thick board), and the depth of just under half the leg's depth. Repeat for the other three legs.

11 Starting with the tabletop joint, clamp each leg, in turn, in a vise if you have one, or if not then to a workbench using clamps. Following the pencil lines, cut out the tabletop joint with a handsaw, repositioning the leg after the first cut to make the second cut easier.

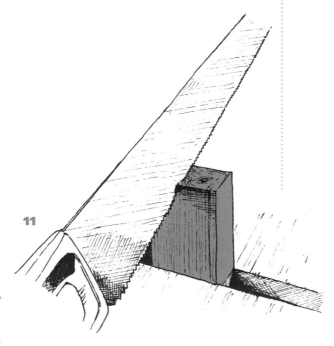

Continued

TIP

• **STEP 14** For a good fit with screws, it is always best to predrill a pilot hole in one of the sections to be fitted together. This makes it easier to drive the screw in straight.

12

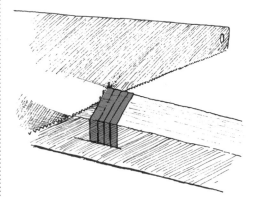

12 Next, cut out the shelf joints with the aid of a technique called kerf cutting, which is a quick and easy method for removing material in a joint like this. To do this, one at a time, clamp the leg in position. Saw down the inside of the pencil lines, then make a series of cuts to the same depth between them.

14 Along with the wood glue, the joints could use a little added strength, which will be supplied by a few well-placed wood screws. The screw for the shelf joint goes through the front of the leg in line with the joint. With the leg securely clamped, drill your hole with the ³⁄₁₆-in/4-mm drill bit.

13

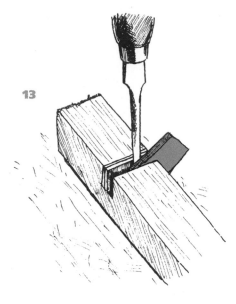

13 When all of the shelf joints have been cut with kerfs, wedge a flat-head screwdriver into the gaps and twist; this should cause the waste material to break away. Use the wood rasp to smooth out the bottom of the joint until it's flat.

14

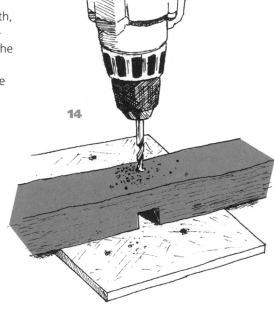

15

15 The screw for the tabletop joint needs to go through the tabletop. Mark a point on the quarter lines drawn on your top, so that when drilled, it will line the screw up with the center of the cutout joint. My legs had 1¼-in-/3-cm-deep cuts, so my screw holes needed to be ⅝ in/1.5 cm from the edge of the disk. Drill these with the ³⁄₁₆-in/4-mm bit.

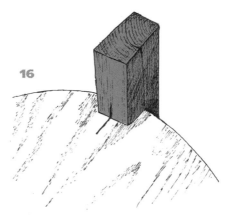

16

16 Perform a dry run to make sure everything fits and adjust as necessary if there are any tight areas. Now, it's time to reach for the wood glue. Starting with the shelf joints and working with one leg at a time, add glue in moderation to each of the three faces of the joint in the leg. Position the leg, lining it up with the quarter lines drawn on the shelf, and secure it with the wood screw.

17 Stand the table on its feet and, after applying glue to all the joints at the top of the legs, fit the tabletop in place, again lining each leg up with its quarter pencil line. Then secure it in place with screws.

18 After the glue has dried, you can sand the table, smoothing down any sharp edges with 120-grit sandpaper.

17

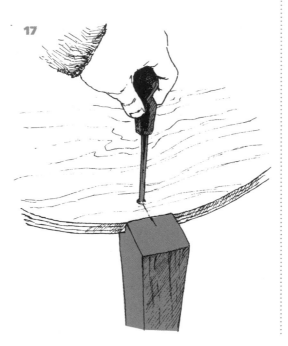

TIPS

- **STEP 16** Before you start to assemble a project, especially if there is glue involved, do what is referred to as a dry run. On this project, you will want to check that the shelf fits easily into its joint; any tightness can be eased with either a wood rasp or 80-grit sandpaper. It's better that these adjustments are carried out before the job is dripping with glue.

  A small, flat stick of scrap wood can be a useful tool for evenly spreading the wood glue.

- **STEP 17** After assembly, and while the glue is still wet, place the table onto a flat, even surface. This will help to make sure the glue dries while the table is flat so it doesn't develop a wobble.

- **STEP 18** If you intend to finish the table with a clear varnish or exterior wood stain, it will be a good idea to remove the pencil marks on the tabletop and shelf with sandpaper. An opaque paint finish, on the other hand, should hide all of your working marks.

The completed breezy table.

(A) *The tabletop rests in the notch, or rabbet joint, made on top of the legs.* **(B)** *Keep the tabletop flush with the top of the leg for a smooth working surface.* **(C)** *The screws can be left exposed, or you can make wider holes into the top section of the pilot holes to sink in the screw heads to hide them.* **(D)** *The dado joint is tailored to the thickness of the shelf.*

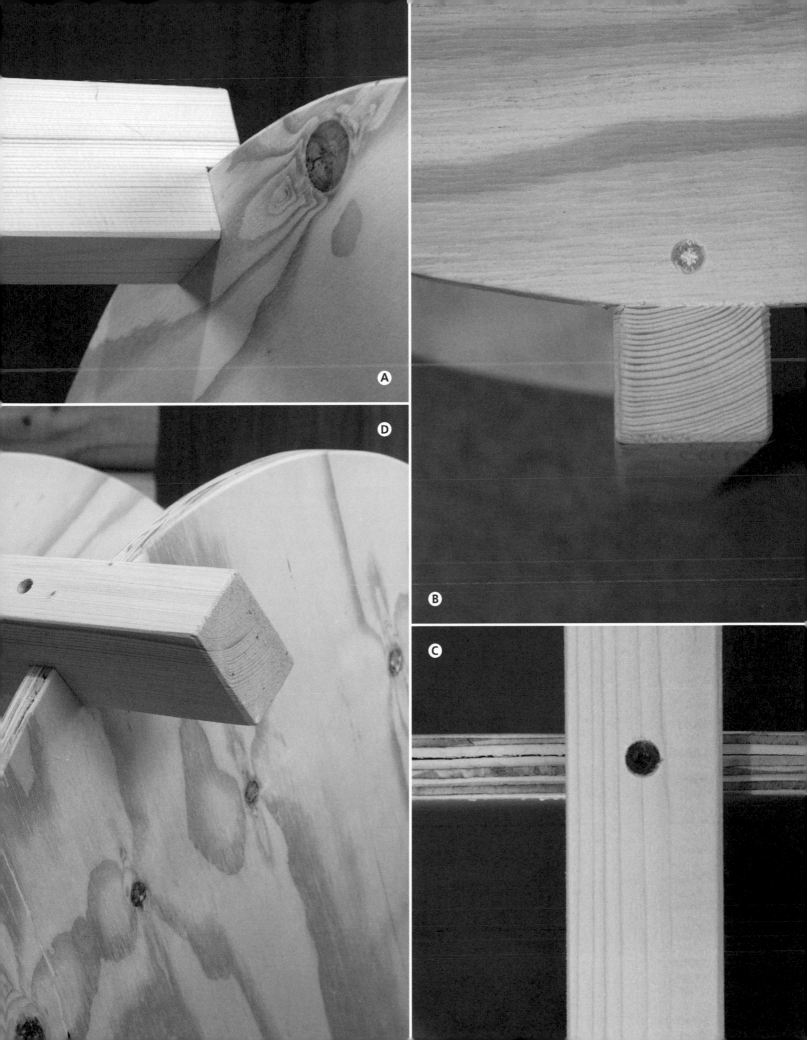

BIRDHOUSE FEEDER

Anything that encourages wildlife into the yard has to be a project worth making, especially if it is as fun to make as this birdhouse feeder. The project doesn't have a back, so it's easy to clean out and fill the feeder. However, to keep the seed, dried worms, or other food from spilling out, you'll need to hang the birdhouse feeder against a flat wall. Start with the simple house design as shown here, then for your next bird feeder, let your imagination run wild and see what you are capable of—you could even re-create your own house.

TOOLS FOR THE JOB

Tape measure and pencil

Clamps

Handsaw

Hand drill with ⅜-in/10-mm and ¼-in/6-mm drill bits

Hole saw

Claw hammer

Wood rasp

FOR AN EASY LIFE

Jigsaw

Cordless drill/driver

EXTRAS

Nails

Wood glue

String

LUMBER CUTTING LIST

½-by-16-by-36-in/
1-by-40-by-91-cm board
(for the front)

½-by-3-by-27-in/
1-by-7.5-by-69-cm board
(for the sides, shelves,
and roof)

¼-by-¾-by-37-in/
6-mm-by-2-by-94-cm
board (for the molding)

TIP

• STEP 2 If you are comfortable using a jigsaw in a confined area, it will make this step go by much more quickly. Keep fingers and the cord away from the blade at all times and always wear safety goggles and a good-quality dust mask.

CHOOSING YOUR MATERIALS

Needing nothing more than a few scraps of wood in its construction and simple enough to be knocked together in a morning, this is a fantastic project to engage any young aspiring woodworkers. You can use manufactured board or solid wood for the main face of the house. I used a reclaimed packing crate, with a thickness of ½ in/1 cm. It is strong enough when put together, yet light enough for hanging from a wall. I made the house front 16 by 36 in/40 by 91 cm, but this is only a suggestion and can be adjusted, if preferred. I made my door opening 3¼ by 4¾ in/ 8 by 12 cm and my window openings 2¾ by 4¾ in/7 by 12 cm.

I've added wood strips as molding, which are a wonderful place to add color detail. You can be creative and add more molding around the door, up the sides, and elsewhere, too, or you may prefer not to use any molding at all. I've used sturdy string to hang the feeder. After exposure to the weather, it may need replacing, so check it occasionally.

If you prefer, you can use this project to create a hanging house for displaying small plants in the windows. Be sure the windows are large enough to accommodate the flowerpots, and make the shelves deeper so they can hold them.

Steps

1 Following the design of the feeder in the photograph and the measurements given above, use the tape measure and pencil to draw the house design on the wood for the front, including the windows and door. With the wood clamped to a work surface, cut out the shape of the house, using the handsaw.

2 Drill a single hole in the center of each window and the door, using the ⅜-in/10-mm bit. This will be large enough to slip in the blade of the hole saw, which you should now use to cut out each opening, starting from the hole and working your way toward the pencil lines.

ASSEMBLY GUIDE

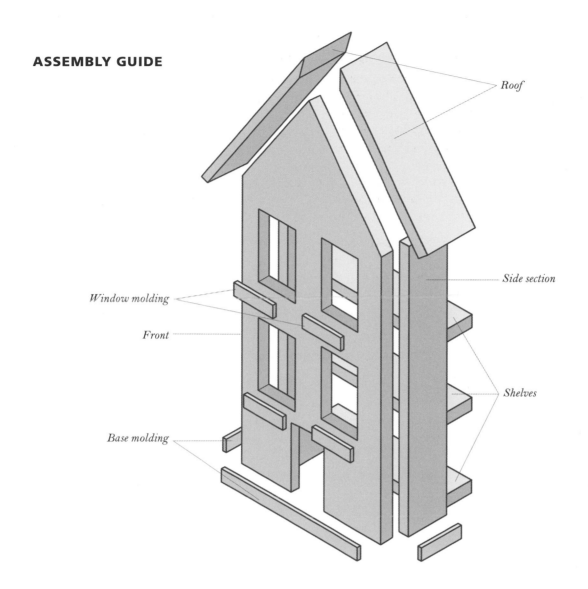

Roof

Window molding

Front

Base molding

Side section

Shelves

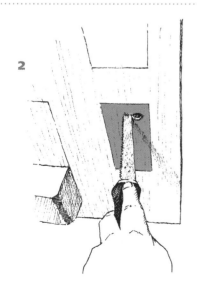

2

③ With the house front, door, and windows cut out, turn your attention to the sides and shelves, cutting the material to a uniform width of 3 in/ 7.5 cm, if necessary. Now, working around three edges of the house front—the bottom shelf and the two side sections—measure, mark, and cut the wood to size, using the handsaw.

Continued

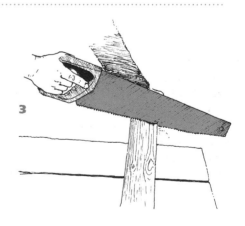

3

TIPS

- **STEP 4** If you want to hide the nail heads that are visible on the house, place the point of a large nail onto the nail's head, then give the large nail a hard tap with the hammer to send the smaller nail just below the surface, leaving a small hole that can be filled and sanded.

- **STEP 7** You can leave the point at which the roof boards meet as a simple butt joint, but when you make the shape of the house front, make sure the peak of the roof is at a 90-degree angle to match.

- **STEP 10** You can decorate your birdhouse feeder in bright colors (perhaps painting the molding in a contrasting color), or simply leave it in its natural state with a clear exterior coating. Whatever finish you choose, your birdhouse will look charming when populated with happy, feeding birds.

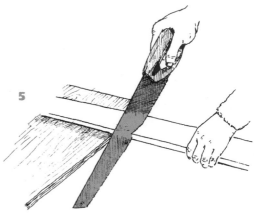

4 Glue and nail the side sections and bottom shelf in place, nailing through the house front into the edges of the boards below. Where the sections butt together with the bottom shelf at the two lower corners, drive two nails through the face of one board into the end of the other board to secure them.

5 The other shelves sit aligned near the bottom of the windows. Measure and mark the length for the shelves, then cut them to size with the handsaw.

6 Dab wood glue on the shelf edges, position them, and nail in place, from the sides of the house into the edges of the shelf. If you're not sure where to place the nails, draw light pencil marks following the edges of the shelf around the sides and front, then erase them later on.

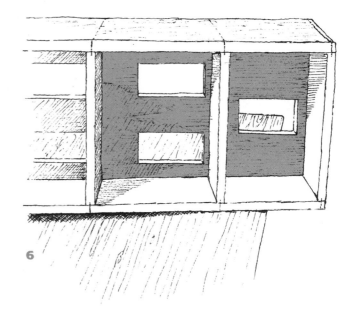

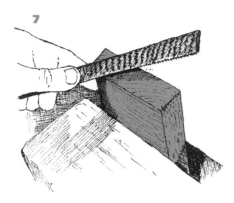

7 For the birdhouse roof, cut two lengths of the 3-in/7.5-cm board a few inches longer than the roof edges on the front of the house. To make a peak to match the roof point on the house front, use a wood rasp to create angles where the boards will butt together.

8 Once you are happy with the angles for the roof peak, measure and mark the length of the boards, allowing for an overhang, then cut them with the handsaw. Now glue and nail the roof pieces in place, nailing through the front into the edges of the roof pieces.

9 Cut ¼-by-¾-in/6-mm-by-2-cm board into strips to add details, such as molding for the windows and around the base of the house, using the handsaw. You can cut straight edges or cut them on an angle for added interest. Simply nail or glue the molding in place.

10 To create a simple way to hang the birdhouse, first drill a ¼-in/6-mm hole at the top of each of the side sections, ½ in/1 cm in from the edge. Run a piece of string through the holes, tying it off with knots at each end. Use the string to hang up the feeder on a nail or hook.

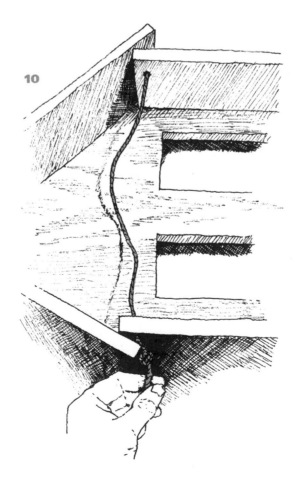

The completed birdhouse feeder.

(A) *The roof is nailed into place into the top edge of the front panel.* **(B)** *The shelving behind the windows and door is for the bird seed.* **(C)** *The roof looks most attractive if it overhangs the front and the* sides of the birdhouse. **(D)** *The string's knot is concealed where the roof overhangs the sides.* **(E)** *When placing the molding below a window, try to keep its top edge flush with the bottom of the window.*

GRAND VIN DE LÉOVILLE
DU MARQUIS
DE LAS CASES
St JULIEN, MÉDOC
12 Blles.
1999

BORDEAUX BEEHIVE

The hobby of beekeeping has increased in popularity in recent years, and it's not just confined to rural locations—today's beekeeper societies can be found in major cities throughout the country. Whether it's the interest in tending to your own colony, the pleasure of tasting home-produced honey, or the friendship that comes from joining a local beekeeper society, once stung (sorry), the beekeeping hobby will grow on you.

One colony will quickly turn into two or three as demand for honey from friends and family increases. This is where the next project comes in: a standard beehive with its different sections, insulation layers, and ventilation holes can be challenging to build, whereas this nucleus, or nuc, beehive is straightforward to make, and a good starting point in the world of beekeeping. It is intended to house a small colony for a few months, but you can also use it as a swarm box or for transporting bees.

TOOLS FOR THE JOB

Tape measure and pencil

Claw hammer

Handsaw

Clamp

Flat-head screwdriver

Wood rasp

Pliers

Hand drill with ³⁄₁₆-in/4-mm and ³⁄₈-in/10-mm drill bits

FOR AN EASY LIFE

Cordless drill/driver

EXTRAS

Nails

Wood glue

LUMBER CUTTING LIST

Two standard wooden wine crates (for the carcass, roof, and side extensions of the beehive)

Ten 1½-in-/4-cm-long ³⁄₁₆-in-/4-mm-diameter dowels (to section the side extension pieces)

Two ³⁄₈-by-¾-by-13⅞-in/ 1-by-2-by-35-cm boards (for the long battens)

Eight ³⁄₈-by-¾-by-2½-in/ 1-by-2-by-6-cm boards (for the short battens)

CHOOSING YOUR MATERIALS

The hardest part of the project will be getting two wine crates. Of course, you can buy them and drink the wine over a responsible period of time, or you could ask for donations from a local wine shop, liquor store, or supermarket. The carcass will be made from one of the wine crates, and the second crate will provide the material for the roof and any extension pieces that you might need. To give the extension pieces a little added strength when secured to the carcass, you'll need some wood dowels.

Most hives are built to hold a standard frame known as a Langstroth, which you should purchase from a beekeeping supplier. This beehive is for eight deep-body Langstroth frames, each having a length of 19 in/ 48 cm, a depth of 9⁹⁄₁₆ in/24.3 cm, and a width of 1⅛ in/2.9 cm, but a small nuc with three to five frames will work, too. It is onto these frames that the bees will create honey, and it will be these dimensions that determine the size of your hive. As luck would have it, the average wine case is just long enough to house a 19-in/48-cm frame. I found most wine boxes come up a little short of the 9⁹⁄₁₆-in/24.3-cm depth the frames require, so the box side sections will have to be extended. Double check this measurement against your own frames to make sure they are the same.

That leaves the hive's width: the crucial measurement in beehive making is ³⁄₈ in/10 mm. This is a bee's width or "space," which refers to the space between each frame and the sides of the frames and hive. A ³⁄₈-in/10-mm gap allows bees to move around freely, yet it also prevents them from constructing comb, which would make it difficult to remove a frame.

Steps

1 The internal depth of your beehive needs to be large enough to fit a 9⁹⁄₁₆-in/ 24.3-cm Langstroth frame flush with the top edge of the box and still leave a bee space of ³⁄₈ in/10 mm between the bottoms of the frame and the box.

Subtract the depth of your first crate from this measurement to determine the width you'll need for the extensions to the side sections. If the crates are of different sizes, use the smaller one as the carcass.

ASSEMBLY GUIDE

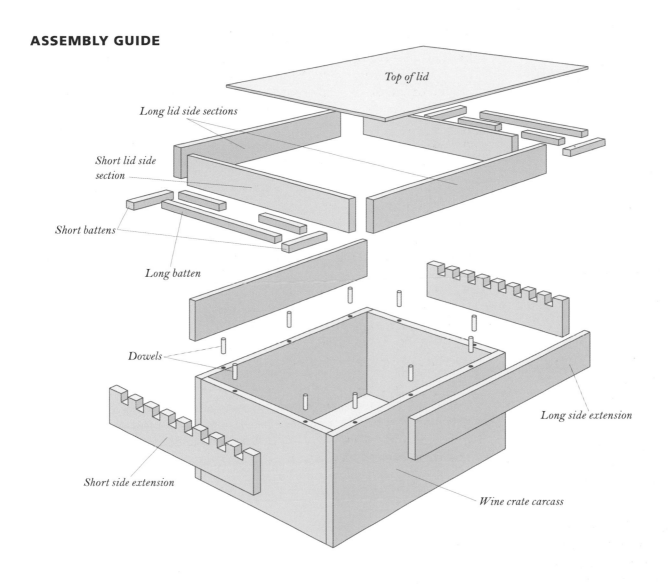

Top of lid

Long lid side sections

Short lid side section

Short battens

Long batten

Dowels

Short side extension

Long side extension

Wine crate carcass

2 Dismantle the second wine crate, using the claw hammer. Using the tape measure and pencil, mark the width of the four side extensions on the dismantled wood, then cut them to size with the handsaw. Align two boards with the long side sections of the first crate, mark where they will need to be cut, then use the right-angle indicator on the handsaw handle to mark perpendicular ends and cut to size. For the two short side sections, mark the distance between the long side sections on the crate and cut to size.

Continued

TIPS

- **STEP 3** The number of notches you make may vary, depending on the size of the crate, but you should have a minimum of three pairs of notches for three frames.

- **STEP 8** If the original size of the wine box is a little too small to use as the lid, add boards from the second crate to extend it, as you did for the sides.

- **STEP 11** I finished the hive in an animal-friendly, nontoxic, weather-resistant varnish.

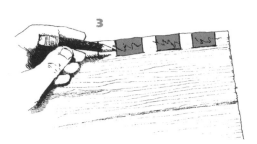

③ Next, make the notches in the short side sections to hold the frames. Each notch should be 1⅛ in/2.9 cm wide and there should be ⅜ in/10 mm between each notch and also between the first and last notches and the adjacent sides of the crate. Use a pencil to mark the notches onto only one short side section. Draw a line at the bottom of the pencil marks at the depth of the hanging lug on the frame, which is normally about ⅜ in/10 mm. Scribble pencil lines into the notches that will be removed.

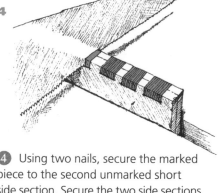

④ Using two nails, secure the marked piece to the second unmarked short side section. Secure the two side sections with the clamp and, using the handsaw, cut on the inside of your pencil lines down to the bottom line. Then cut a few slots between your side lines. This is known as kerf cutting.

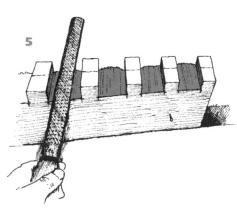

⑤ When all of the marked notches are cut out, slip a flat-head screwdriver between the sides and pry the two apart. Work the screwdriver between the kerf slots and twist to break away the waste wood. Clean any ragged kerfs with a wood rasp, and you should be left with two castlelike sides ready to fit to the hive.

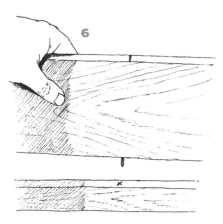

⑥ You'll need ten dowels to secure the side extensions to the wine crate. Here is a simple trick to make the dowels match up. Mark on the crate edges the position the dowels need to be: three evenly spaced along the long sides and two along the short sides. Tap in a nail partway at these marks, then snip off the nail heads with a pair of pliers. Now line up the side sections, one at a time, with the corresponding crate sides and give them a tap with a hammer. You will now have a small hole as a guide for your drill bit. Remove the nails with the pair of pliers and you'll have matching guide holes in the crate.

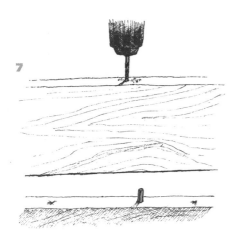

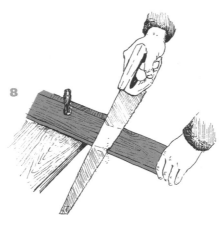

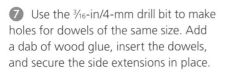

7 Use the ³⁄₁₆-in/4-mm drill bit to make holes for dowels of the same size. Add a dab of wood glue, insert the dowels, and secure the side extensions in place.

8 The bees will need ventilation, and this is provided for in the construction of the lid. The lid has sides that overlap the body of the beehive, and it rests on battens to allow for a ³⁄₈-in/10-mm bee space all around the hive. To create the top of the lid, trim the bottom of the second wine crate, using the handsaw, so that it is ¾ in/2 cm wider and longer than your hive.

9 To create the lid's side pieces, using the handsaw, cut two 2¼-in-/5.5-cm-wide boards from the second wine crate the same length as the long side edges of the lid. Fit them in place with wood glue and nails. Cut two more 2¼-in-/5.5-cm-wide boards, but to fit between the two long sides you just fitted. Secure them in place with wood glue and nails, adding extra nails to secure the corners.

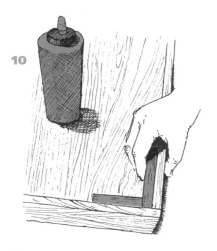

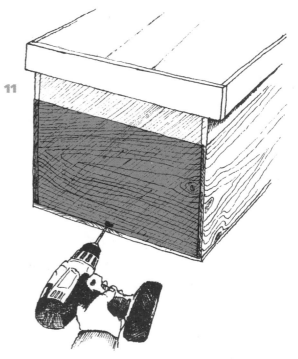

10 Flip the hive lid upside down. Cut two ³⁄₈-by-¾-by-13⅞-in/1-by-2-by-35-cm long wood battens the same length as the inside of the short sides of the lid and secure them in place, with glue, in the joins between the lid and short sides. Next cut eight ³⁄₈-by-¾-by-2½-in/1-by-2-by-6-cm short wood battens. Glue two of the battens into each of the lid's corners, so that they are flush with the edge and butting against each other. These strips provide the hive with a gap for a healthy air flow.

11 Before sliding the frames in place and setting the lid on, you need to provide the bees with a door. In the center of one of the short side sections, just above the hive's base, drill three holes side by side, using the ³⁄₈-in/10-mm drill bit. Wiggle the drill until the three holes become one slot.

(A) *The lug of the Langstroth frame sits in the notch in the side extension.* (B) *The side extension pieces sit flush with the sides of the crate.* (C) *The battens provide a gap around the lid for ventilation.* (D) *The size of the crate will determine the number of frames it can hold.* (E) *Making an elongated hole at the bottom of the crate provides a door for the bees.*

The completed Bordeaux beehive.

GRAND VIN DE LEOVILLE
DU MARQUIS
DE LAS CASES
ST JULIEN , MÉDOC
12 Blles.
1999

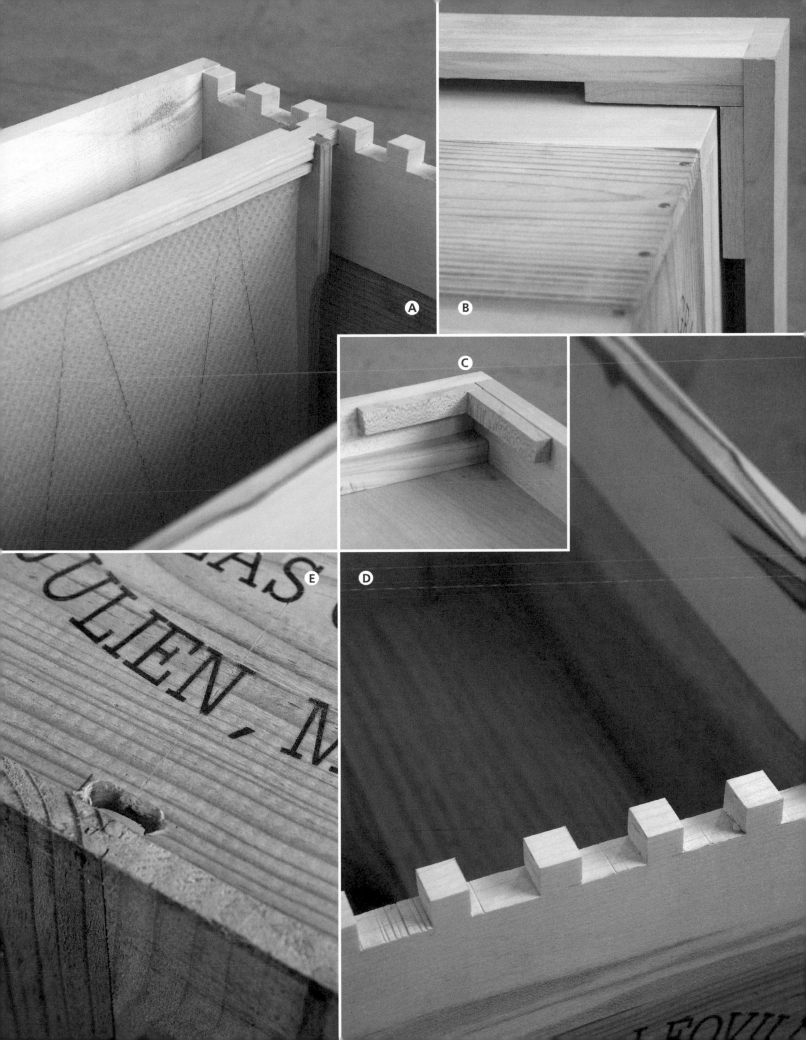

SHAKER PLANK BENCH

When it comes to creating furniture that highlights the natural beauty of wood, it's hard to better the objects made by the Shaker community. Sparse in elaboration, their handiwork relies on a combination of practical design, solid craftsmanship, and an understanding of how wood works, creating a legacy of classic pieces.

This bench is based on one such Shaker design. As well as being versatile, it is easy to make. You can make a smaller bench with two sets of legs, or you can increase it in size with additional sets. It makes the perfect companion to the X-Frame Dining Table featured on page 113.

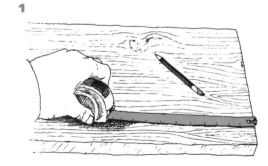

5 HOURS

TOOLS FOR THE JOB

Tape measure and pencil

Handsaw

Straightedge or length
of straight board

Clamps

Hand drill with 1¼-in/3-cm
spade bit and ³⁄₁₆-in/4-mm
drill bit

Sandpaper, 120-grit,
and woodblock

Screwdriver

Claw hammer

FOR AN EASY LIFE

Cordless drill/driver

Jigsaw

EXTRAS

Wood screws

Nails

LUMBER CUTTING LIST

Three 1¼-by-9-by-17¼-in/
3-by-23-by-43.8-cm boards
(for the legs)

Two ¾-by-3½-by-36-in/
2-by-9-by-91-cm boards
(for the side rails)

Seven ¾-by-5-by-12-in/
2-by-12-by-31-cm boards
(for the seat planks)

TIP

• For a unique look, collect
together odd boards, some
with different paint colors
or just different shades of
natural wood, and mix
them up.

CHOOSING YOUR MATERIALS

This is not a project that requires a lot of materials. Many of the odd leftover boards from other projects will be enough to make you a bench. Decide on the height, depth, and length for the bench, thinking first about where you might use it to make sure it will fit the space. As a general guide, a standard seat height is about 18 in/46 cm and a comfortable, stable seat depth is about 12 in/31 cm. The bench with three sets of legs shown here is 35 in/89 cm long. To make sure your bench is strong enough, plan on having a set of legs every 18 in/46 cm. The legs will require lumber no thinner than 1¼ in/3 cm. I was able to cut my three from an old oak dresser door. For the height of the legs, subtract the thickness of the seat planks from the total height you want the bench to be. You'll also need to subtract the width of each of the two side rails from the width of the legs. If you want to create an overhang, with the seat planks extending beyond the legs and side rails—as I did, with a ¾-in/2-cm overhang on each side—subtract this amount from the width of the legs, too.

The two side rails connect the sets of legs together and give the bench its rigidity. The side rails do not need to be too thick, and something in the region of ¾ in/2 cm will be suitable. They should be around 3½ in/9 cm wide, and cut them to length so that they will be 1½ in/4 cm less than the finished length of your bench.

The choice for the seat planks depends on what lumber is available. You can choose boards because you find they have a striking grain pattern that will be an interesting feature in the finished product. Or you may intend to paint the bench in a bright color, so any old boards will do for the seat. Whatever your choice, the boards should be a minimum of ¾ in/2 cm thick for a sturdy seat.

Steps

1 Using the tape measure and pencil, measure and mark the set of legs on the boards. After subtracting the thickness of the seat from the finished height for the bench and the width of the side rails and overhang from the final depth for the bench, for my 18-in-/46-cm-high, 12-in-/31-cm-deep bench, my legs were 17¼ in/43.8 cm high and 9 in/23 cm wide. Cut the legs with the handsaw.

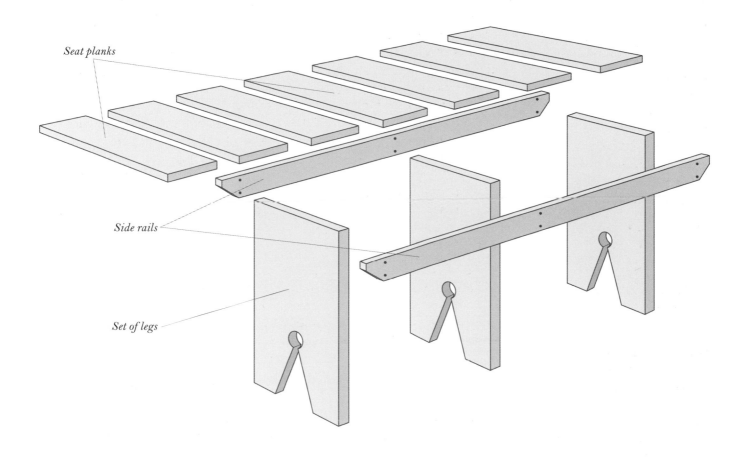

Seat planks

Side rails

Set of legs

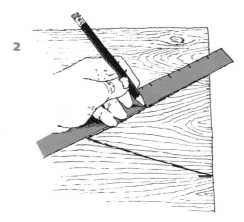

2 On a set of legs, from each bottom corner, measure in 3 in/7.5 cm along the bottom edge of the board and make a pencil mark at this point. Now, measure halfway across the bottom edge of the board, then measure up by 6 in/15 cm and make a pencil mark. Using the pencil and straightedge, draw lines to connect the three pencil marks, forming a triangle. Repeat for each set of legs.

Continued

2

TIPS

- **STEP 3** If possible, clamp the work piece to a surface before drilling and place a scrap wood board behind it. This will help prevent "break out" of the wood on the reverse of the leg.

  Always wear safety goggles when drilling.

- **STEP 4** You will find it quicker and easier to cut out the triangles with a jigsaw if you have access to one.

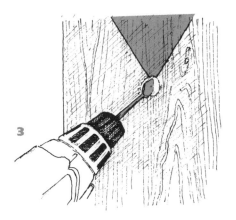

3 Fit a 1¼-in/3-cm spade bit into a handheld or electric drill and drill a hole with the edge aligned with the tip of the marked triangle. Repeat for each set of legs, making sure you position the tip of the drill bit in the same spot in relation to the tip of the triangle.

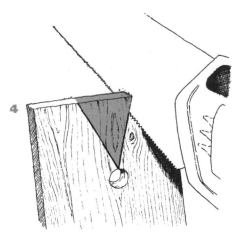

4 When all the holes are drilled, using the handsaw and following your pencil marks, cut out the triangles. Sand all the edges of the legs with a piece of 120-grit sandpaper, being careful to remove any sharp edges.

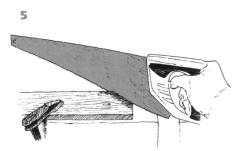

5 To make angle cuts on the ends of the side rails, make a pencil mark ¾ in/2 cm down one short edge and 3 in/7.5 cm along the long edge that is farthest from the first mark. Draw a pencil line between the two marks and cut off this corner with the handsaw; repeat on all of the rail ends, making sure the angles are all marked in the correct direction before cutting them.

6 You'll need to make pilot holes on the side rails to secure the set of legs to them. On each rail, from the bottom of each of the angles just cut, measure ¾ in/ 2 cm along the edge and draw a pencil line from the bottom to the top of the rail. Now, measure in 18 in/46 cm and make pencil lines for the middle set of legs (or for a longer bench, continue to make pencil lines a maximum of 18 in/ 46 cm apart for each set of legs). Using a ³⁄₁₆-in/4-mm drill bit, drill two holes on each of the pencil lines, about ½ in/ 1 cm for the edges.

7 It is now time to assemble your bench. Working on a flat surface, line up the set of legs on their sides, with the triangles all at the bottom. Lay one side rail on the legs so that it is flush with the top edges of the legs. Line the drilled holes up with the center of the legs' edge and fasten with 2¼-in/6-cm wood screws. Carefully flip the assembly over and repeat with the second rail.

8 The basic frame is now complete, but your bench will need a seat. Measure the depth of the bench and add 1½ in/ 4 cm for an overhang, then measure and mark the boards for the seat planks and cut them to size with the handsaw.

TIPS

- **STEP 9** To keep the nails in line when fitting, draw a light pencil line on the seat, following the rail below, then erase the line after you finish nailing down the planks.

After you have applied a paint or stain finish, apply a varnish to seal it against the elements.

9 Now simply lay the seat planks, with a ¾-in/2-cm overhang on each edge, and secure them to the frame with 1¾-in/4.5-cm nails into the side rails below.

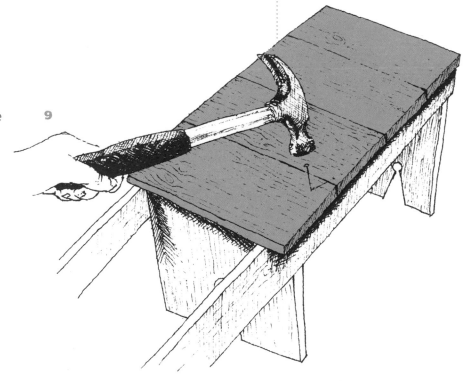

The completed
Shaker plank bench.

(A) *Weathered or aged planks can be just as attractive as new lumber.* **(B)** *For a neat appearance, try to keep the holes in the legs at the same position in relation to the triangles.* **(C)** *Contrasting grains add to the finished look.* **(D)** *Check how the seat planks will look side by side before fastening them to the side rails.*

WALL-MOUNTED LADDER RACK

I finally had to face up to the fact that my much-loved wood extension ladder was long past its best days. Each time I ascended the ladder, listening to every heart-stopping creak as I stepped on the next rung, I knew that this was a warning sound of its—and possibly my—demise. Well, if it couldn't be used as a ladder anymore, I would have to come up with other uses for it. One idea that came to mind was this storage rack. Suitable for the yard, workshop, or garage, it can be adapted to organize and store an endless number of things that ordinarily end up being left and lost around the place.

TOOLS FOR THE JOB

Tape measure and pencil

Screwdriver

Handsaw

Sandpaper, 80- and
120-grit, and woodblock

Clamp

Claw hammer

Hand drill with ½-in/12-mm,
⁵⁄₁₆-in/8-mm, and ¼-in/
6-mm drill bits and ⅛-in/
3-mm metal bit

FOR AN EASY LIFE

Cordless drill/driver

Wood rasp

Utility knife

Level

EXTRAS

Wood glue

Nails and wood screws

Glass screw-top jars

LUMBER CUTTING LIST

One ladder section

Two ½-by-6¼-by-8¾-in/
1-by-16-by-22-cm boards
(for the middle box)

Two ½-by-6¼-by-8¼-in/
1-by-16-by-21-cm boards
(for the sides, middle box)

Four ½-by-4¼-by-8¾-in/
1-by-11-by-22-cm boards
(for the narrow boxes)

Four ½-by-4¼-by-8¼-in/
1-by-11-by-21-cm boards
(for the sides, narrow boxes)

One ½-by-6¼-by-7½-in/
1-by-16-by-19-cm board
(for the shelf; optional)

½-in-/1-cm-diameter
dowel (for the pegs)

Two 5-in 2×2/5-by-5-by-12-
cm blocks (for the mounts)

CHOOSING YOUR MATERIALS

For this project, you can use either an extendable ladder or a stepladder that, when disassembled, can be made into two racks. The project here explains how to make one rack—simply repeat for a second rack. If you don't want to make two racks, why not use a section to make the Ladder Plant Stand on page 45? Remember that you don't have to hang the ladder rack horizontally—it will work just as well vertically. Although any square cut ends on your ladder legs can be left as they are, rounding them off looks more attractive and will make the rack a little safer.

These ladder racks will be more useful if they have some deeper storage. For this purpose, I chose a selection of old wooden wine crates that I had been collecting to make storage boxes. Okay, they weren't the right size, but it was easy to knock them apart with a claw hammer and use all that perfect ½-in-/12-mm-thick planed lumber—just remember to remove the nails with the hammer before using the wood. If you want to add pegs, you'll also need some ½-in-/12-mm-diameter dowels from a hardware store or, if you want a handicraft look, you can trim to size some wood material you may happen to have around. I decided to make one of the boxes deeper and add a shelf to another box, but you can alter the arrangements on your ladder shelf to suit your own needs.

Yet another form of storage I mounted to one of my ladder racks was two glass jars. These are ideal for seeds, odd screws, or anything you want to store and see. Choose jars with metal screw-top lids.

The ladders are supported by woodblocks fastened to the wall. This will make it easier to take the ladders down, if needed—for example, if you want to paint the walls.

Steps

1 You may need to trim the length of the ladder section to fit the available space. Using the tape measure and pencil, measure the space where you want to hang the ladder section and mark the measurements on the ends of the ladder. Using the screwdriver, remove any metal hardware on the ladder holding sections together. Now cut the ladder legs at the pencil marks, using the handsaw.

2 Using scrap lumber or cardboard about the width of the ladder's legs, draw and cut out a rounded-off shape for the ends of the ladder. Use it as a template to transfer the shape to each ladder end, using the pencil. Using the handsaw, trim off the corners.

ASSEMBLY GUIDE

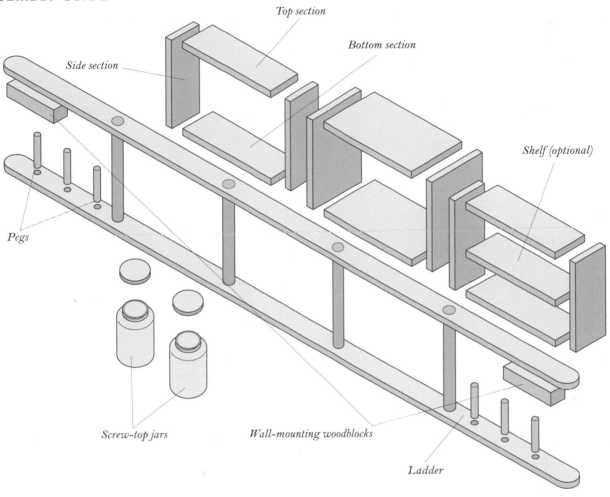

Top section

Bottom section

Side section

Shelf (optional)

Pegs

Screw-top jars

Wall-mounting woodblocks

Ladder

2

3 Round off the remaining wood to your pencil line, blunting any sharp edge as you work, using either 80-grit sandpaper wrapped around a scrap woodblock or the wood rasp.

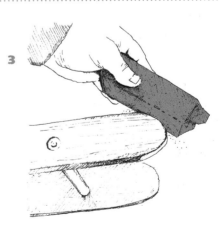

3

Continued

TIPS

- **STEP 7** On my ladder racks, I decided to fit a shelf into one of the boxes, but this is an optional step. With the boxes glued together, I marked the box's width on two pieces of wood, and then cut and fitted them in the same way as I assembled the box.

  Clean away any excess glue with a damp rag.

- **STEP 10** When drilling wood, always wear safety googles.

  To prevent the wood from splitting as you drill, clamp a piece of scrap wood to the side of the ladder leg where the bit will exit.

  You can reattach the metal hardware to the ladder racks to use as hooks to hang things from. Put them wherever you think they will be convenient.

- **STEP 15** If you want to paint your ladder racks, it's better to do so before securing them to the wall. I decided to leave mine in their original paint-splattered character.

4 Line up a piece of ½-in/1-cm board to a gap between two ladder rungs, and mark the gap on the wood with the pencil. All the gaps between the rungs should be identical, but you may want to double check before cutting all of the box material. Using the handsaw, cut two lengths to this size for each box you want.

7 You can now assemble the boxes. For each box, stand two side sections on end and run a line of wood glue on the edge. Lay a top section on top and nail to the sides with three or four nails that are about twice the thickness of the box material. With the top section in place, flip the box over and fit the bottom section in the same way.

5 Position two of the lengths into the top and bottom of the rung gap. Taking another piece of ½-in/1-cm board and, using a pencil, mark onto it the distance between the box top and bottom; this will be the size of the box sides. Using a handsaw, cut the same quantity as you have tops and bottoms.

6 With the box sections cut out, decide on how deep you want the boxes to be. I decided on two side boxes at 4¼ in/11 cm deep and a middle box at a deeper 6¼ in/16 cm. Mark the sections with the measurements for the depth, clamp them to a work surface, and cut to size along the pencil lines with a handsaw.

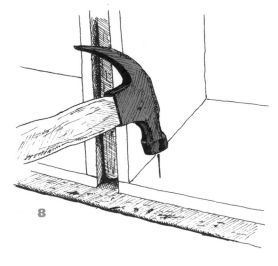

8 When the glue is dry, sand the boxes with 120-grit sandpaper, then fit them into the ladders so that they are flush with what will be the back of the rack. Using the claw hammer, fasten each box in place with nails through the top and bottom of the box and into the ladder's legs.

9 To add pegs for hanging items from, using the pencil, mark a line on the outside of the ladder sides where the pegs will go. The line should be centered along the width of the ladder's legs, on the outside edge.

10 Divide this line into the number of pegs you aim to fit. I went for three pegs on the end of each rack with a gap of 1¾ in/4.5 cm between them. Using the ½-in/12-mm drill bit, drill out your holes.

11 If you prefer, you can drop in on the local lumberyard or hardware store and pick up a length of ½-in-/12-mm-diameter dowel for your pegs. Or make your own: trim a few blocks of wood to roughly ½-in/12-mm square, using the handsaw or wood rasp. With the utility knife, whittle the corner edges away from the wood until the pegs will sit tightly into the holes drilled.

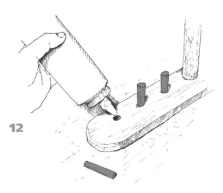

12 When the dowel fits, trim it to about 2 in/5 cm and dull the sharp top edge by rounding it off with 80-grit sandpaper. Squeeze a small amount of wood glue into the holes and tap the pegs in with the claw hammer until flush with the back of the ladder leg. Repeat for the other dowels.

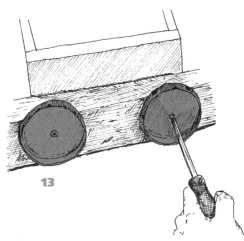

13 To attach the jars with metal screw-top lids to the ladder, clamp the lid to a piece of scrap wood and drill through the center with the ⅛-in/3-mm metal drill bit. Position the lid on the ladder frame and screw it in place with a wood screw.

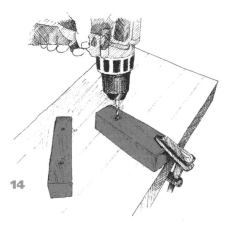

14 For the wall-mounting woodblocks, drill two 5/16-in/8-mm pilot holes for the screws that will attach the woodblocks to the wall. Then use the ¼-in/6-mm drill bit to drill holes in the top leg of the ladder for the screws that will secure the ladder to the woodblocks.

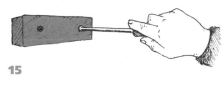

15 With a buddy holding the ladder in place, use the pencil to mark the location for each woodblock clearly on the wall. (If you have access to a level, you can make this job more accurate.) Measure and mark the position for pilot holes, then drill them. Depending on the type of wall you want to fix your rack to, you will need to insert some type of wall plug or anchor, then screw the woodblocks in place. My buddy held the rack in place again while I secured it in place with long screws.

The completed wall-mounted ladder rack.

(A) *Inserting the pegs all the way through the ladder enables them to hold heavier objects.* **(B)** *When attaching the screw-top lids to the ladder, make sure the back edge doesn't go beyond the ladder, so the rack can sit flush to the wall.* **(C)** *The box fits snugly into the gaps created by the ladder's rungs and legs.* **(D)** *Boxes can be inserted in gaps side by side, but make sure the nails are staggered so that there's no danger of them hitting one another.* **(E)** *The sides and top and bottom of each box are both glued and nailed in place for strength.*

PERFECT
PLANT
ARBOR

A friend of mine asked me to come up with an idea for the bare, uninspiring yard of her new house. What she really wanted was a few trees to give the space some height and interest. Unfortunately, with all the expense of house renovation work, her budget wouldn't stretch to planting mature trees. So a more cost-effective solution was required. I had made this project with scrap wood, but walking around her yard, I saw a pair of worn-out screen doors stacked against a wall, waiting to be taken away with the garbage. The screen itself was torn, the hinges were useless, but the lumber was sound—and it hadn't been painted. Combined with the pile of old floorboards lying nearby, we had the basic materials for a classic arbor.

TOOLS FOR THE JOB

Tape measure and pencil

Handsaw

Hand drill with ⅜-in/
10-mm and ³⁄₁₆-in/4-mm
drill bits

Screwdriver

Clamps

Triangle (optional)

Flat-head screwdriver

Sandpaper, 80-grit,
and woodblock

Claw hammer

FOR AN EASY LIFE

Jigsaw

Cordless drill/ driver

Surform plane

EXTRAS

Wood screws

Nails

LUMBER CUTTING LIST

Four 2-by-3-by-78-in/
5-by-7.5-by-198-cm boards
(for the side pieces of
the side frames)

Four 2-by-3-by-12-in/5-by-
7.5-by-31-cm boards (for
the top and bottom pieces
of the side frames)

Two 1-by-5-by-48-in/
2.5-by-12-by-120-cm
boards (for the roof rails)

Five 1-by-5-by-32-in/
2.5-by-12-by-81-cm boards
(for the roof cross pieces)

Twenty 30 in 1×2/
2.5-by-5-by-76-cm boards
(for the trelliswork)

CHOOSING YOUR MATERIALS

Using a pair of screen doors will get this project off to a quick start, and it's just one example of how you can reclaim objects to make something else. If you don't have screen doors, you might have frames from an old folding screen or something else. However, even without reclaimed objects for the frames, this project is still within reach to the inexperienced woodworker. Making up the side frames yourself is not a huge challenge, and the steps here describe how to make them. I used 2×3/5-by-7.5-cm boards.

For the trelliswork, you can use thin boards, wood dowels, small branches from trimming a tree, or even bamboo canes. For my trellis, I used some lengths of 1×2/2.5-by-5-cm stock leftover from another job. For the roof rails and cross pieces, you will need lengths of lumber, such as 1×5/2.5-by-12-cm boards; old floorboards are ideal.

Steps   2

❶ If you have screen doors, go on to step 5; otherwise, start by making the side frames. First, using the tape measure and pencil, measure and mark four 2×3/5-by-7.5-cm boards to the height you want your arbor to be, to make the side pieces. Next, measure and mark the same lumber for the top and bottom pieces. The length of these will determine the depth of the arbor, but about 12 in/31 cm is a good guide. Cut the eight lengths of wood at the pencil marks, using the handsaw.

❷ To mark the screw positions, place the four long side pieces on their edges. Using one of the short pieces, stand it on end on one of the long pieces, flush with the end, and draw a pencil line. Repeat for each end of each of the four long side pieces. You now have the area marked in which to place the screws.

Continued

ASSEMBLY GUIDE

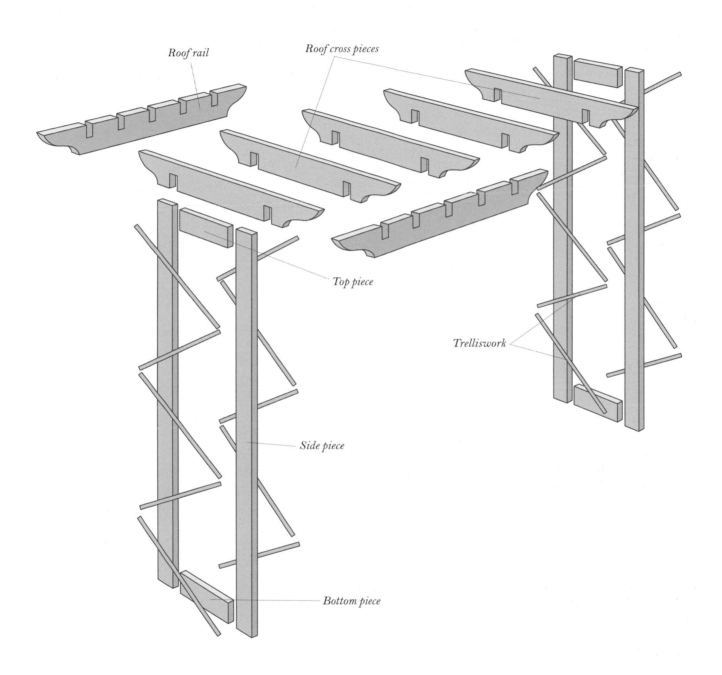

Roof rail

Roof cross pieces

Top piece

Trelliswork

Side piece

Bottom piece

- **STEP 3** When you need to drill a hole to a specific depth, lay the drill bit next to a ruler or tape measure and wrap a piece of masking tape around the drill bit, marking the point to stop drilling.

- **STEP 4** Rubbing the screw over a wax candle before driving it in will make the task a lot easier—and avoid that distressed duck sound.

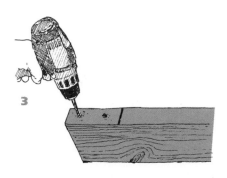

③ Without getting too close to either the pencil line or the end of the wood, drill two ⅜-in/10-mm holes into each end of all the side pieces, stopping at about the depth of the screw head. Now, using the smaller ³⁄₁₆-in/4-mm drill bit, starting in the center of the ⅜-in/10-mm hole, drill straight into it to the length of the screw. This hole will let you "countersink" the screws, so the heads are flush with the work.

④ For each side frame, lay out the long side pieces and short top and bottom pieces on the floor and, with the screwdriver, drive long wood screws through the countersunk pilot holes into the short pieces, making sure the screws are long enough to go at least 1½ in/4 cm into the side pieces. Put the side frames aside.

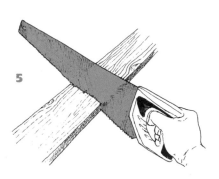

⑤ Now, turn your attention to the roof of the arbor. Calculate the width the arbor needs to be; for example, if it is to span a pathway in the yard, you will need to allow for this and a little extra on each side for some leeway. Add 14 in/36 cm onto this measurement to give the roof of the arbor a good 7-in/17-cm overhang on each side—my arbor needed to be 4 ft /120 cm wide. With the tape measure and pencil, measure and mark two 1×5/2.5-by-12-cm boards to this size for the roof rails, then cut them with the handsaw.

⑥ Now, measure the width of the side frames, and add 14 in/36 cm onto this measurement, again to allow for the overhang. For my arbor, my side frames were 18 in/46 cm, so I cut boards to 32 in/81 cm. Now, as in step 5, measure, mark, and cut five 1×5/2.5-by-12-cm boards to this size for the cross pieces.

7

8

7 Shaping the ends of the boards will add a touch of style to the arbor. If you have access to a jigsaw, give the ends a soft curved shape; alternatively, cut a long sloping angle, using the handsaw. Whichever shape you choose, the shape should end about 5 in/12 cm from the end of the board. Draw the shape on both ends of each roof piece, using a template to keep the shape consistent (see the Tip, right), then use the jigsaw or handsaw to cut out the shapes.

8 Place the two long rails for the roof on top of each other so that they are flush all around. Secure them temporarily together with clamps or a couple of nails. Place them on your work surface so that they stand on edge, with the shape you have cut on the ends facing down. Using the tape measure and pencil, measure and mark 9 in/23 cm from each end, then measure back toward the end of the board the thickness of a roof cross piece, so you have a pair of pencil marks. For example, if the cross piece is 1 in/2.5 cm thick, then you will have one pencil mark at 9 in/23 cm from the end and one 8 in/ 20 cm from the end.

9

9 Next, you'll need to add another three pairs of pencil marks, evenly spaced between the two sets of marks you've just added. These marks are the center points for the roof's cross pieces, so you'll need to make a pair of marks at each one that matches the thickness of a cross piece, as in step 8. For example, if the cross piece is 1 in/2.5 cm thick, measure and mark ½ in/12 mm from each side of the center point. You should now have five sets of pencil marks in total.

10

10 Measure and mark all five of the short cross pieces 9 in/23 cm in from each end in the same way as the rails in step 8, measuring the thickness of the roof's rail back toward each end of the board and making a pencil mark.

Continued

TIPS

- **STEP 7** To make sure the curve or angle is the same on each arbor roof piece, make a template of the shape. You can use a scrap from the lumber boards, a piece of paper, or cardboard to make a template, then use the template to draw around with a pencil.

  When operating the jigsaw, always wear safety goggles, and make sure the blade will not come into contact with the cord or fingers.

- **STEP 9** To help you with your marking, when equally dividing the space between two end points, divide it by one number greater than the number of marks you want to make; so for this project, to make three evenly spaced sets of marks, divide the space between the two sets of pencil marks at the ends by four.

TIP

• **STEP 11** Treat yourself to a proper carpenter's pencil. It will give you clear, thick lines to work with, won't break on rough lumber, and will make you look like a master at your craft.

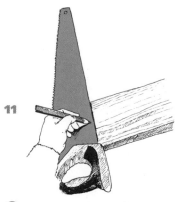

11 Next, at each set of pencil marks on the two long roof rails, you'll need to mark the depths for what will be cross-lap joints. Many handsaws have a handle with a miter square built in to make accurate right-angle marks; alternatively, use a triangle. Continue the pencil lines on the edge over to the face of the board, then using the tape measure, draw a perpendicular line to connect them about three-quarters of the way down from the edge.

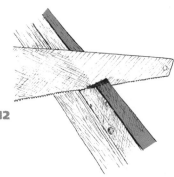

12 Using the handsaw, cut out the waste inside the joints. As neatly as you can, start by cutting on the inside of each vertical pencil line all the way down to the three-quarter mark. Then cut another three lines between these, again down to the three-quarter mark; this is known as kerf cutting. (You'll now see the benefit of clamping or nailing the long boards together in step 8: you only have to carry out the marking and cutting operation once.)

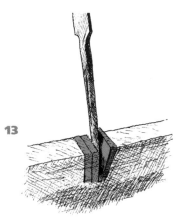

13 With all the joints sawed, wedge a flat-head screw driver between the kerf cuts and twist it so the kerfs break away, leaving a ragged bottom to the joint. Clean it with either 80-grit sandpaper or a Surform plane.

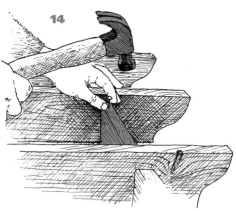

14 It's time to put the roof together. Start by slipping the short cross pieces into the corresponding cross-lap joints in the two long rails. You can loosen any tight joints by sanding with the 80-grit sandpaper. Once everything fits in place, hammer long nails diagonally through the joints to add strength.

15 Now join the roof to the side frames. Set the frames on edge on the floor, then if your measurements are correct, the arbor roof should slip over the top of the frames. An extra pair of hands will be helpful. Fasten the side frames in place with a few long wood screws. The arbor can now stand up.

16 It's back to the numbers! Divide the length of the side frames by five and mark four points on the two front edges. These are the reference points for positioning the arbor's trelliswork.

TIPS

• **STEP 17** If you space the trellis pieces carefully at right angles, only the top and bottom pieces will need both ends trimmed, because you can butt one end against the sawn piece.

I applied three coats of a preservative wood stain for the finish, but you could paint your project if you prefer.

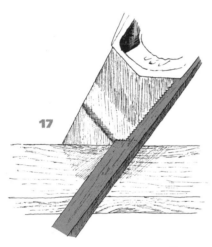

17 Using the pencil marks as a guide, attach the trellis pieces in a zigzag pattern on each face of the side frames. The ends will need to be cut at an angle, and you can do this by placing the piece in position, marking a pencil line along it aligned with the edge of the side frame, then cutting with a handsaw. Work one at a time, nailing each piece to the face of the side frame.

18 With some help from a buddy, set the arbor in place in the yard. You can use metal rods with hooked ends, available from hardware stores, to secure the arbor frame in the ground.

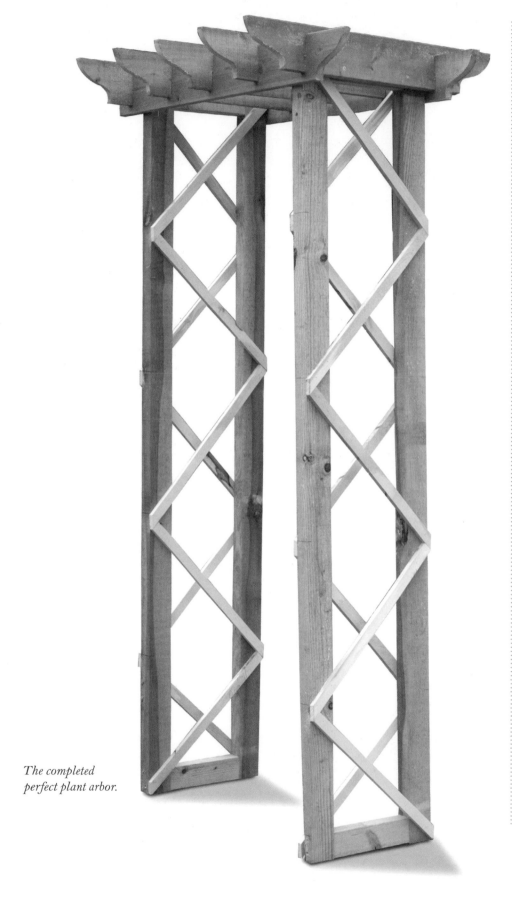

The completed
perfect plant arbor.

(A) *Using a template and the jigsaw makes it easy to make consistent curves at both ends of each of the cross pieces and the rails.* **(B)** *The trelliswork is secured on both faces of the side frames.* **(C)** *The cross pieces fit snugly on top of the roof's rails.* **(D)** *The roof of the arbor fits neatly over the side frames.*

X-FRAME DINING TABLE

If, like me, you enjoy using your outdoor space to invite family and friends over, cook some food, and have a party, you will know the importance of a good, solid table—something that can handle the pounding of a big get-together and still look great. Just imagine the sense of pride you'll feel when everybody is admiring the table that you made with your own hands. Follow these simple steps and you will learn a few wood-working tricks, have some fun along the way, and end up with a unique table that is handsome enough to reside indoors or out, and that will last for years.

✔ 1½ DAYS

TOOLS FOR THE JOB

Claw hammer

Tape measure and pencil

Handsaw

Hand drill with
⁵⁄₁₆-in/8-mm drill bit

Flat-head screwdriver

Wood rasp or
Surform plane

Sandpaper, 80-grit
and 120-grit

FOR AN EASY LIFE

Cordless drill/driver

Electric sander

EXTRAS

Wood screws

Wood glue

Nails

2 wing nuts, bolts,
and washers

LUMBER CUTTING LIST

One ledge-and-brace door
or five 1-by-7¼-by-72-in/
2.5-by-18.5-by-183-cm
floorboards (for the
tabletop)

5 ft 4 in/1.6 m of ½-by-2-in/
1-by-5-cm boards (for the
battens)

19 ft/6 m of 3-by-3-in/
7.5-by-7.5-cm boards
(for the legs and center rail)

CHOOSING YOUR MATERIALS

Let's start with the tabletop, because it's the top that will establish the dimensions of the base frame. The perfect solution is to find an old ledge-and-brace door (sometimes called a batten door). They are often used on sheds, barns, and other outdoor buildings and are traditionally constructed with boards on the back of the door—two of which run at angles, forming a "Z" pattern—and a plain front made up from long, vertical boards. One place to look for a door like this is the local junkyard or reuse center. If you are in luck and find one, don't be deterred if it had a hard life and shows some signs of wear and tear. This is just character that, when cleaned up, will give the tabletop an attractive, well-used heirloom appearance.

If, however, that perfect door is too elusive to find, some extra work will be involved, but the finished results will be just as impressive. Instead, you'll need reclaimed floorboards. These should be long enough to get the length of table you require, and there should be enough that, when set side by side, you have a good top width.

The last thing you want will be a wobbly table, so for this reason, it's important to choose thick, good-quality lumber for the X-frame legs. I would say nothing less than 3 by 3 in/7.5 by 7.5 cm will do. If nothing of this size turns up from your usual sources, there is only one option: a trip to the local lumberyard. Ask for 13 ft/4 m of 3-by-3-in/7.5-by-7.5-cm board (or 4×4/10-by-10-cm board will do); this will cover the X frames, and you will also need a length of the same stock for the center rail, which should be the same length as the table.

As an approximate guide, 36 in/91 cm is an average width for a dining table, so if making this project with floorboards, you would need five 7¼-in/18.5-cm boards.

Steps

① If using a door, move on to step 2. For floorboards, use the claw hammer to pry out any old nails. Measure out and mark the length of the table on the boards, then cut to size with the handsaw. Shuffle the floorboard pieces around until the grain and color look in harmony with each other. Keeping this formation, flip the floorboards over.

ASSEMBLY GUIDE

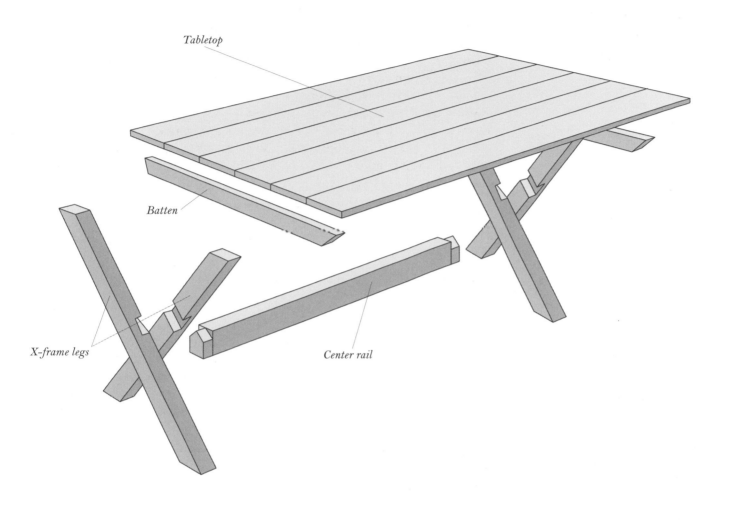

Tabletop

Batten

X-frame legs

Center rail

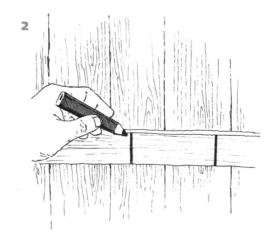

2 Cut two ½-by-2-in/1-by-5-cm battens 4 in/10 cm shorter than the tabletop's width, using the handsaw. Position a batten at each short end of the tabletop, 2 in/5 cm in from the long edges. Using the tape measure and pencil, mark pilot holes centered in the width of the batten at the center of each floorboard or board of the door.

Continued

TIPS

- **STEP 3** The pilot holes for the screws may look too large, but they provide flexibility so that the top of the table can move as the wood expands and contracts. Without this tolerance, the wood may split. Be sure the head of the screw is larger than the hole.

Before screwing the battens down, check that the screws being used are long enough to go at least halfway into the tabletop, yet not so long that they come through the face of the top.

- **STEP 4** Mark the legs with a number sequence. As the joints are cut and legs assembled, you will be able to keep track of what goes where.

- **STEP 5** Scribbling in pencil lines on the parts of a piece that need to be removed will ensure you cut at the right places. It may seem obvious here, but getting into the practice of doing this will avoid mishaps on other projects, too—as many woodworkers have discovered, it's all too easy to make the wrong cuts.

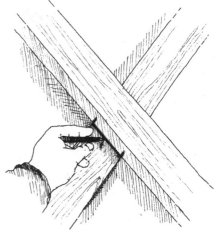

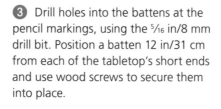

3 Drill holes into the battens at the pencil markings, using the ⁵⁄₁₆ in/8 mm drill bit. Position a batten 12 in/31 cm from each of the tabletop's short ends and use wood screws to secure them into place.

4 With the tabletop facedown on the floor, work out the size and joint angles of the four legs for the two X frames. Cut four lengths of the 3-by-3-in/7.5-by-7.5-cm board to 39 in/1 m, using the handsaw. One at a time, position two boards in an X on the table, with the outside corners placed 1¼ in/3 cm in from the ends of the batten. Using the tape measure, check that the distances from the center of the X to the point where each leg touches the batten are identical. Using the pencil, draw a pair of lines on each board, one on each side of the X; repeat for the other frame.

5 Now make a half lap joint for each pair of legs. It's simple and strong, and once mastered will be useful for future projects. Your handsaw should have a handle that enables you to mark out right angles. Use it to continue the lines drawn onto the two side faces of the leg, halfway down the sides. Measure down on these new lines half the width of the wood and draw a horizontal pencil mark between them. Each leg of the X frames should now have the joints marked out on their opposing faces. Scribble pencil lines in the area where the joint will be.

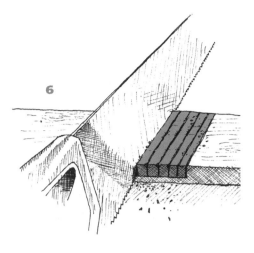

6 With the handsaw, cut a vertical line just on the inside of your pencil marks, down to the horizontal halfway mark you have made. Now cut lines between these about ¼ in/6 mm apart; this is known as kerf cutting.

7 Using the flat-head screwdriver, wedge it between the kerfs and give it a twist; this should break out the wood until the joint is clear.

TIP

- **STEP 9** If a joint is on the tight side when you are assembling the legs, try giving it a tap with the hammer, but put a scrap piece of wood between the hammer face and the workpiece to avoid making marks.

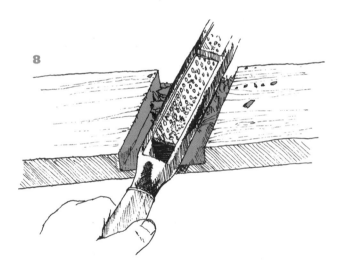

8 Clean out any ragged parts of wood left behind with a wood rasp or Surform plane, leaving a flat bed to the joint that is in line with your halfway pencil mark.

9 Try fitting together the pieces of each joint; any tightness can be eased with the rasp or 80-grit sandpaper. When satisfied with the fit, add a little wood glue to all the joint faces that meet and push them together. Tap two nails through the joint to hold it while the glue dries. Use a damp cloth to wipe away any excess glue.

Continued

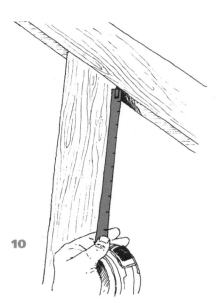

10

TIP

• **STEP 12** Balancing the X end of the center rail to mark the joint can be a bit of a juggling act. Either employ an extra pair of hands to help, or use a clamp to secure the center rail to your work bench, making it more stable for accurate marking.

10 When the glue is dry, measure and mark where to make angled cuts at the ends of the X-frame legs, based on the height you want for the table. Starting from the same point on each lap joint, measure down the outside edge of the legs toward the bottom ends and mark with the pencil. Using a piece of wood with a straight edge aligned at the two marks at the bottom of the frame, draw a pencil line along it. Repeat for the top ends of the frame. As long as your measurements are accurate, the angles on the frame will be flat, so the table won't wobble. Using the pencil lines, cut the ends with a handsaw.

11 One more part is needed to keep the table rigid, and that is its center rail that runs between and connects the two X frames. Place the X-frame legs in position, tight to the battens, and measure the distance between them. Add 2 in/5 cm to this measurement to give the rail a 1-in/ 2.5-cm overhang on each end. Now cut the rail to this size, using the handsaw.

12 To get the center rail to fit snugly in the X frames, sit the end of the rail in the bottom notch of an X-frame joint. Copy the two angles of the legs onto the rail end with the pencil. Measuring in from the end of the rail, mark 90-degree angles at the depth of the leg plus the 1-in/2.5-cm overhang, where the diagonal lines meet the sides. Cut along each side of the rail, following the V on the rail end, then cut from the end to the first cuts to remove the wedges.

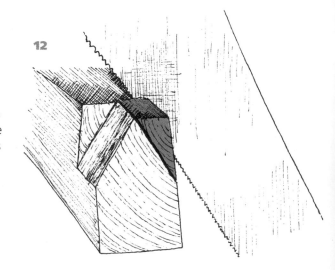

12

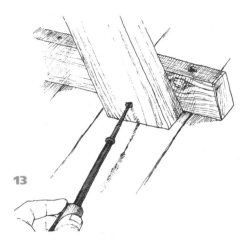

13 It's a good idea to have a table that can be dismantled when needed; it helps when storing it, and when it's time to revive the finish. For this reason, I decided to make my rail/leg connections with bolts and wing nuts. Holding the leg/rail assembly in place, drill a $5/16$-in/8-mm hole through the center of both and fit a bolt of the same gauge with washers at each end. Now you can screw the X-frame legs to the battens attached to the tabletop's underside.

14 With the table frame assembly together and upside down, it's an easy job now to go around it to remove any sharp edges with some 120-grit sandpaper. When done, flip the table over onto its feet, and get the first look at your handiwork.

15 Wherever your top has come from, it will probably be in need of a good sanding. Start with 80-grit paper and finish with 120-grit paper. If it's not too bad, you could get away with just 120-grit paper. It will be a tough one to do by hand, so use an electric sander, if you can get hold of one.

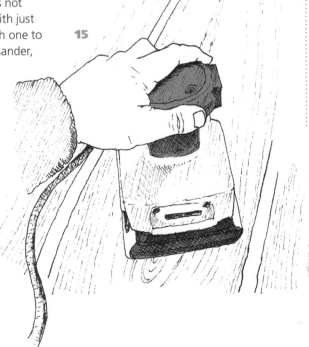

TIPS

- **STEP 15** For the best results, always sand in the direction of the wood grain. Sanding across the grain will leave scratches that affect the quality of any transparent finish applied.

When sanding, whether by hand or machine, always wear a good-quality dust mask.

When it comes to giving the table a finish, you have several choices. If you prefer the wood look, and you anticipate the table will be exposed to a lot of weather, try one of the many tough exterior-grade varnishes, maybe even something designed for the marine trade. If, however, the table will be sheltered, maybe even spend time indoors, a good-quality oil finish will really bring out all the beauty of the wood. As for the frame, it could be left natural and treated as above, or why not add a bit of color in the form of either an exterior wood stain, or an exterior paint shade.

The completed X-frame dining table.

(A) *You'll need long bolts to go through the center rail and into the X frame.* **(B)** *Driving the screws from the leg to the batten hides them from view.* **(C)** *The center rail connects the two X frames, providing strength and stability.* **(D)** *For a steady table, make sure the legs are snug against the battens under the tabletop.*

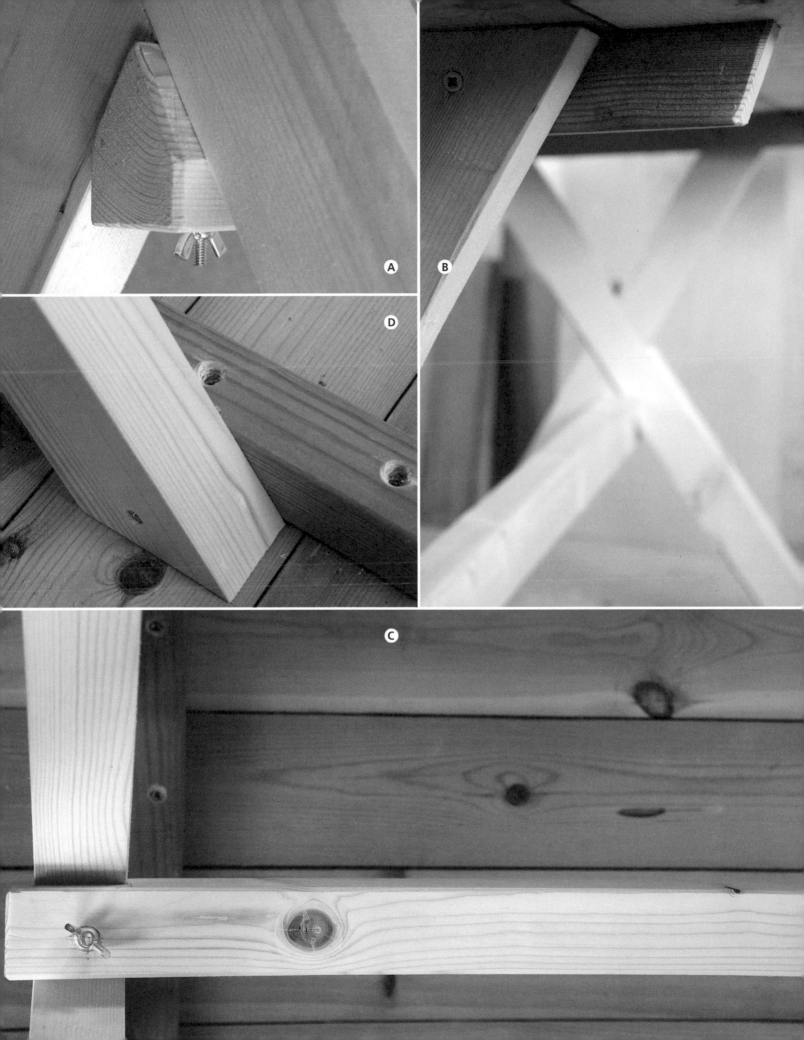

CHUNKY LAMINATED BLOCK STOOLS

After many a happy weekend spent creating wonderful wooden objects for yourself and your friends' outdoor spaces, if you take a look around the workshop all you may see are large quantities of seemingly useless scraps of wood, only fit for the wood stove. Well think again. What you have there are the raw materials to make these handy stools. Use them for tables, flowerpot stands, or even beside the bed to keep your milk and cookies on. Make them as large or as small as you want, round or square in shape. As a variation, I made one up using the branches from a tree that was in need of pruning. Whatever you decide, the building principle is the same—and simple.

TOOLS FOR THE JOB

Tape measure and pencil

Handsaw

Hand drill with ⅜-in/10-mm and ³⁄₁₆-in/4-mm drill bits (optional)

Screwdriver

Claw hammer

Surform plane

Sandpaper, 80- and 120-grit, and woodblock

FOR AN EASY LIFE

Cordless drill/driver

Electric sander

EXTRAS

Wood glue

Screws

Nails

LUMBER CUTTING GUIDE

Four 2-by-2¾-by-22-in/ 5-by-7-by-56-cm boards (for the legs)

Approximately 30 assorted scrap woodblocks or logs

TIP

- **STEP 2** If you don't have a flat, level floor, work on top of an unwarped sheet of manufactured board.

CHOOSING YOUR MATERIALS

Collect a pile of scrap wood and pull out four pieces that are about the length you want for the stool's height. A good stool height is 21 in/ 53 cm, but you may want to choose a different height for your own needs. These lengths will be the legs, so choose lengths that are thick, at least 2 in/5 cm square. They don't have to be the same thickness—in fact, the stool will be better if they are not. When choosing the scraps or logs to form the seat, consider the contrast and hues of the colors and the wood grain and how they work together.

The end grain, as found on the top of the stool, is the hardest part of the wood, so it takes a lot of sanding to get a result you'll be happy with. However, the payback will come as you apply the first coat of your chosen finish—a well-sanded, end-grain top is truly a thing of beauty.

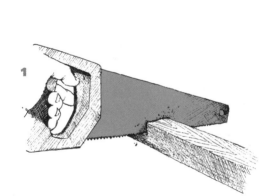

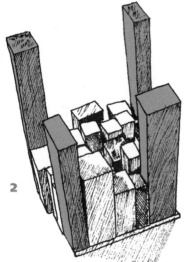

Steps

1 Using the tape measure and pencil, measure and mark the height of the stool on the four lengths chosen for the legs. Using a handsaw, trim them down so that they are equal in length.

2 Place the four legs on their ends about where you want the corners of the stool to be and at about the size you want. Now, work out like a jigsaw puzzle how you want the collection of scrap wood pieces to fit together to make the stool.

Continued

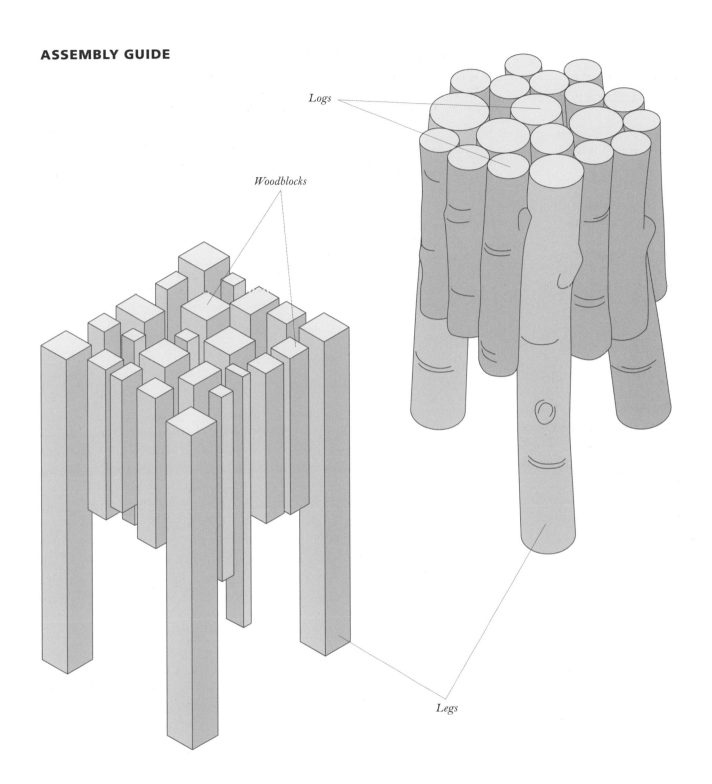

Logs

Woodblocks

Legs

TIPS

- Before you get started, make sure you have the claw hammer, screwdriver, nails, screws, and wood glue ready and close at hand. For the best results, once you start assembling this project, you should keep working without taking breaks.

- STEP 3 Applying the glue for the project can be a bit messy, so it can be a good idea to work on a ground cloth or other material. Also wear rubber gloves, because some types of glue can irritate skin on contact.

It will help when fitting the screws if you predrill the first section to be fitted. Start by using a ⅜-in/10-mm bit to drill a hole the same depth. Then drill straight through with a smaller ³⁄₁₆-in/4-mm bit.

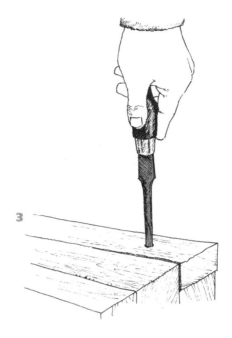

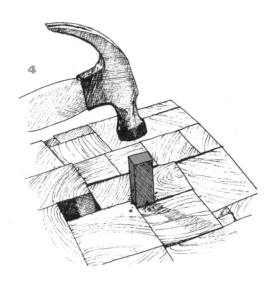

3 Starting with the first leg, dismantle the mocked-up puzzle and, one by one, glue and screw together each piece. It will be easier to assemble if the pieces are laid on one side. Try to keep the ends that will make the seat aligned as much as possible. For the legs, screws are best for a stronger joint; however, on smaller scrap pieces, nails will be better for holding the wood while the glue dries.

4 Once the final main pieces are fitted together, flip the stool over onto its legs. You will probably find a few gaps in the top. No problem: look in the stack of wood scraps for small pieces of wood to fill the holes. If necessary, trim them with a saw or take off some wood with the Surform plane; a tight fit is preferred. Add a little glue to the hole and use the claw hammer to tap the wood infill piece into the gap; it's okay if it protrudes. Let the project sit overnight until the glue dries.

5 When you look at the project the next day, you should find a dry, solid little stool in need of a cleanup. The first task is to trim off any protruding infill pieces with the handsaw. Lay the saw flat on the top and cut them flush with the rest of the wood.

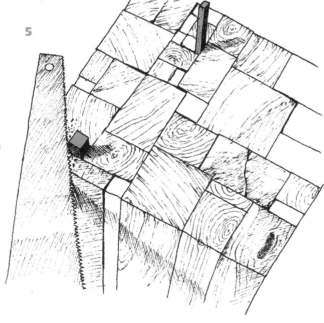

6 If you are lucky enough to own or have access to an electric sander, you will appreciate it now; if you don't, then this is where the hard work starts. Working first with 80-grit sandpaper and then 120-grit sandpaper, give the stool a good working over, removing any excess glue, sharp edges, and splinters.

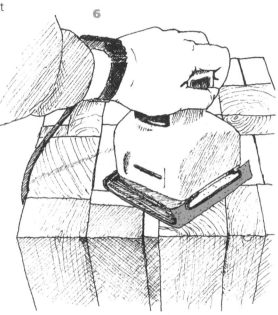

ALTERNATIVE PROJECT

You can make your stool from logs and branches by following the same steps for assembling the stool with scrap pieces. However, because the wood will be green—that is, it will have a high moisture content— it will not take a finish well, so leave it in its natural state.

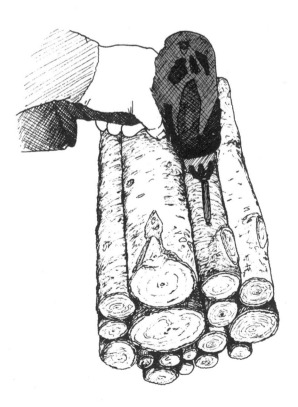

TIPS

- **STEP 6** Sanding is no fun, but the more effort you put into it, the better the end results will be. Most types of glue will block any finish you apply from absorbing efficiently, leaving unsightly patches in the applied varnish or oil, so make sure you sand off any glue.

Whenever sanding with a power tool or by hand, always wear a good-quality dust mask.

Choose your finish to suit the environment where it will end up. If it is to live outside and you want to show off all the hard work you put into sanding that top, choose either a flexible exterior high-gloss varnish or a weather-proof oil coating. If you desire a more subtle finish (the sanding didn't go so well), try a penetrating wood stain— this will give the stool a color to contrast with its surroundings.

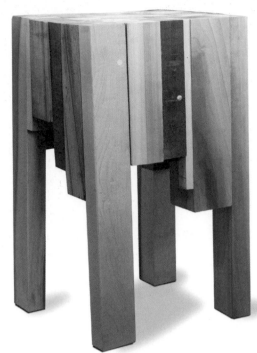

The completed chunky laminated block stools.

(A) *The logs for the seat can be a similar length— the choice is yours.* **(B)** *When working out the fit of the scrap pieces, consider how the colors and grains will work together.* **(C)** *The stool is more interesting when the scrap pieces are of various lengths.* **(D)** *Make sure the exterior edges are kept aligned as much as possible for a neat, crisp appearance.*

TREASURE CHEST STORAGE

One thing that I am often being asked to do is to create furniture for storage. Be it inside or outside the home, we are constantly looking for more ways to store our stuff. This storage chest project has the capacity to hold plenty of equipment, it looks good, and is a real hit with children. If you're building the chest for the kids, get them to paint it to provide their own special finishing touch. You can make the chest more easily by building it with a flat top—which has the advantage that it can double as a seat—but the rounded top gives the chest much more character.

TOOLS FOR THE JOB

Tape measure and pencil

Handsaw

Sheet of paper

Scissors

Hand drill with ³⁄₁₆-in/4-mm, ¹⁄₁₆-in/2-mm, and ¾-in/2-cm drill bits

Screwdriver

Claw hammer

Surform plane

Straightedge

Sandpaper, 120-grit

FOR AN EASY LIFE

Jigsaw

Electric sander

EXTRAS

Wood glue

Wood screws and nails

Hinges and link chain

Rope

LUMBER CUTTING LIST

Two 1-by-21½-by-34-in/ 2.5-by-55-by-86-cm boards (for the front and back panels)

Two 1-by-21½-by-22-in/ 2.5-by-55-by-56-cm boards (for the side panels)

Assorted lengths of 1¼-in/ 3-cm board (for battens)

Nine 1-by-2¾-by-34-in/ 2.5-by-7-by-86-cm boards (for the lid slats)

Two ¾-by-3-by-35½-in/ 2-by-7.5-by-90-cm boards (for the plinth)

Two ¾-by-3-by-24-in/ 2-by-7.5-by-61-cm boards (for the plinth)

One ¼-by-22-by-32-in/6-mm-by-56-by-81-cm board (for the bottom panel)

CHOOSING YOUR MATERIALS

The proportions of your treasure chest will depend on the wood you have at your disposal. I made mine 18 by 24 by 34 in/46 by 61 by 86 cm. All of the material for the chest came from a discarded pine wardrobe. The front and back panels were the wardrobe doors, both side panels—which need to be higher than the front and back panels for the lid—came from one side of the wardrobe, and the other side of the wardrobe supplied the slats for the lid. The slats should be about 1 in/2.5 cm thick and of a narrow enough width (mine were 2¼ in/6 cm) to keep them relatively tight to the curve of the side panels. The ¼-in-/6-mm-thick backboard of the wardrobe made the perfect bottom for my chest.

For the chest to have a lid that opens and closes, you will need some hinges. I recommend using brass butt hinges (I used 3-in/7.5-cm hinges); the brass is good outdoors and a butt hinge is easy to fit. A chain will keep the lid from flipping back too far and damaging the hinges.

Steps

❶ Looking at the lumber you have, sketch out a simple drawing of the chest you can make and make a cutting list of the components you'll need. Use the cutting list for this project as a guide to help. Working through your list, usie the tape measure and pencil to measure and mark the components onto your wood.

❷ Using the handsaw, first cut out the front and back panels of the chest. To check that each panel is square (meaning they each have four right angles), use the tape measure to measure the distance from the top right corner to the lower left corner. Now check the distance from the top left corner to the lower right corner. If the panel is square, these two measurements should match.

Continued

ASSEMBLY GUIDE

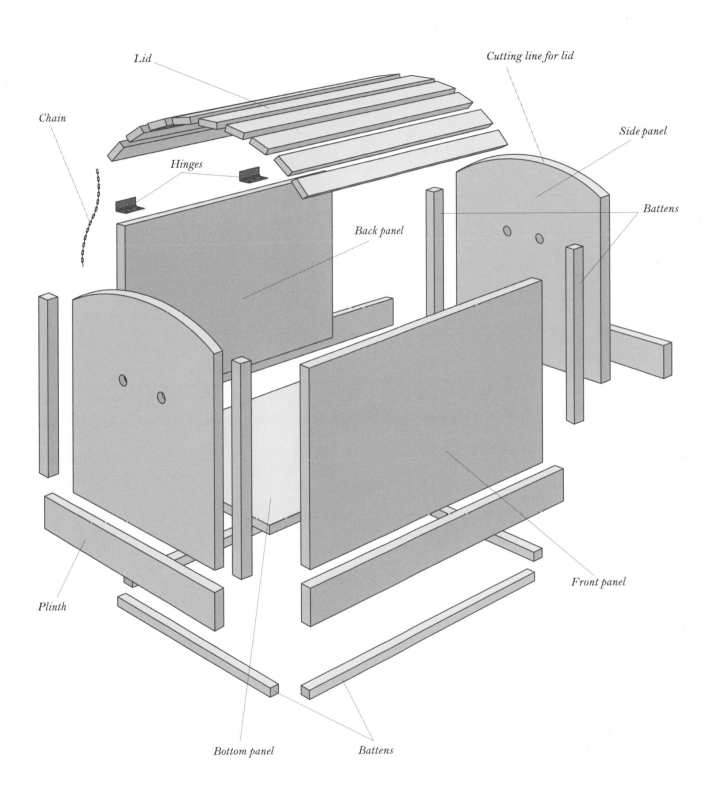

Lid

Cutting line for lid

Chain

Side panel

Hinges

Battens

Back panel

Plinth

Bottom panel

Battens

Front panel

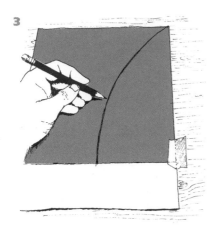

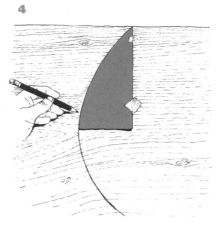

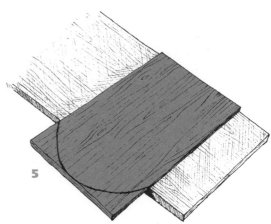

3 Decide on the curve of the lid based on the dimensions of the side panels. Make a template of the curve on a sheet of paper of the same width. From one edge of the paper, draw a horizontal line that is half the width of the side panel. Then, by eye, draw a curve starting on the line at the edge of the paper up to a height that gives the curve a shallow, soft line; on my chest, this worked out at 3½ in/9 cm.

4 When you are satisfied with the curve, cut it out with a pair of scissors, then use the paper template to transfer the curve onto the side panels, tracing around it with the pencil, then flipping over the template to create the two halves of the semicircular shape. Save the paper template.

5 One at a time, line up the top of the front panel with the lower end of the curve you have drawn on the side panels. With the panels held together in this position, mark on each board for the side panels the bottom edge of the front panel. You now have the measurements for the side panels and can cut them to size with the handsaw; however, if you have the jigsaw, use it for the curves.

6 To join together the four panels, you will need to make four battens from 1¼-in-/3-cm-square board. Make them the same length as the height of the front and back panels. Using the ³⁄₁₆-in/4-mm drill bit, make a pair of drill holes through two adjacent faces of each batten. Make the first drill hole 1½ in/4 cm down from the top of the batten, then the second one of the pair on the adjacent face, 2½ in/6 cm down. Continue to make pairs of pilot holes every 4 in/10 cm, starting from the bottom pilot hole in the first set. The reason for this will be obvious in step 12—it's to keep the screws clear of a cutting line.

7 One at a time, after running a line of wood glue along the face of one batten, fasten it along an inside vertical edge of the side panels until all four battens are secured to the side panels. Lay the back panel flat on the floor, with the inside surface facing upward. For each side panel, apply more glue to the adjacent edge of the batten and secure into place with wood screws so that the side panel is flush with the side edge and the bottom of the back panel. After applying more glue to the battens, lay the front panel on top of the free edges of side panels, and secure it into place with wood screws.

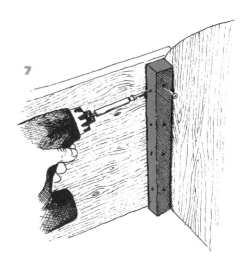

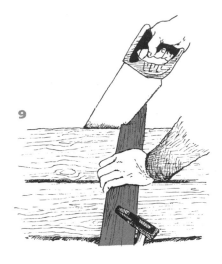

8 To stop "pieces of eight" from falling out, the chest needs a bottom. It's not the time to fit it in place now, but it is a good time to nail in place wood battens around the inside of all the panels, sitting flush with the bottom edge. Measure and mark the length for the two front and back battens, cut them to size with the handsaw, and nail in place with a claw hammer. Now repeat for the battens along the side panel. Let the glue dry.

9 Meanwhile, make the slats for the lid. Using the paper template, work out how many slats you will need to cover the lid evenly. Draw various widths onto the template to find a size that will fit best. Armed with this measurement and using the length of the front panel, start measuring, marking, and cutting the slats with the handsaw. My slats were 2¾ in/7 cm wide and 34 in/86 cm long.

10 Clean the cut edges of the slats using the Surform plane. At the same time, add a slight chamfer (an angled edge) to help the slats fit more snugly together. If done correctly, the top surface of the slat will be slightly wider than the bottom surface.

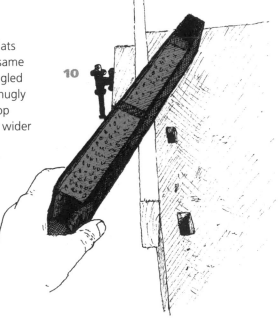

Continued

- **STEP 5** The easiest way to cut the curves in the side panels is by using a jigsaw. However, if you only have the handsaw, use it to cut off the corners next to the pencil marks in the curve until you are close enough that the final shape can be smoothed with a Surform plane.

- **STEP 7** Have a damp rag on hand to wipe away any excess wood glue before it dries.

- **STEP 9** If you use the handsaw for cutting the slats, make sure you use long, slow strokes to avoid damaging the wood when cutting long pieces to a thin width.

When using the jigsaw, keep fingers and the cord away from the blade at all times, and always wear safety goggles and a good-quality dust mask.

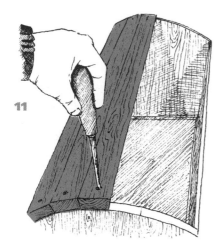

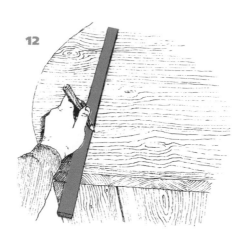

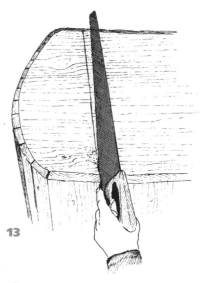

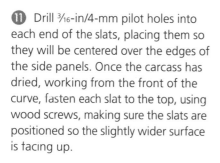

11 Drill ³⁄₁₆-in/4-mm pilot holes into each end of the slats, placing them so they will be centered over the edges of the side panels. Once the carcass has dried, working from the front of the curve, fasten each slat to the top, using wood screws, making sure the slats are positioned so the slightly wider surface is facing up.

12 Standing back from the handsome storage chest, you might notice that you can't get in it. It's time to slice off the top. Measuring 5 in/12 cm down from the bottom of the curve, mark a line around all four sides—this height should avoid your sawing into the screws used in the side battens in step 7. Measure down in several places and draw straight lines using the straightedge.

13 This is one of the few occasions where the handsaw is a better choice of cutting tool than the jigsaw because you want to keep the cut as straight as possible. Following the pencil line slowly, cut around the chest. Sand down the cut edges with a sheet of 120-grit sandpaper until you have a smooth, flat finish.

14 It's now time to fit the bottom panel. Lay the material for the panel on the floor and set the chest on top. With a pencil, draw around the inside edges of the chest panels onto the material. The battens will be in the way, so remove the chest and add the width of the bottom battens to the material. Cut out the panel with the handsaw. Next, cut notches in the corners so the bottom panel can fit around the side battens. Now drop the bottom panel into the chest through the top, where it will settle onto the horizontal battens below. If you want, nail the bottom in place with a few nails; however, this is not necessary.

15 To give the storage chest a more robust look, fit a plinth around the bottom edge of the chest. You can make it in a variety of different sizes. On mine, I used some ¾-by-3-in/2-by-7.5-cm boards. Cut two lengths the width of the side panels, and fasten them in place with glue and nails. Then measure the length of the chest including the side plinths, and cut two lengths to this size and fasten in the same way.

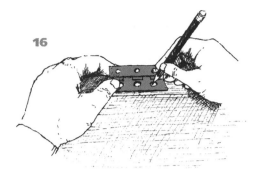

16 To fit the hinges for the top, measure in about 3½ in/9 cm from each end of the back edge of the chest lid, mark a pencil line, then measure in the width of your hinge and make another pencil line. Set the hinge, with the pin part facing outward, between these lines, and mark the hinge holes with a pencil. Using the ⅟₁₆-in/2-mm bit, drill pilot holes for the hinge screws. Repeat the operation on the back edge of the chest carcass.

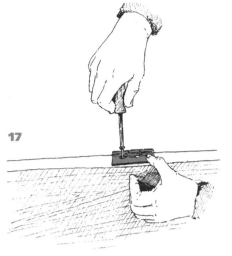

17 Screw the hinges into place on the lid, then with some buddy help if you have it, line up the hinge with the holes in the carcass and fasten with the screws.

TIP

- **STEP 19** Once the chest is complete, it's time to decide on an appropriate finish. If paint is not your thing, and you used some attractive lumber to make the chest, you could finish it with a few coats of an exterior-grade varnish.

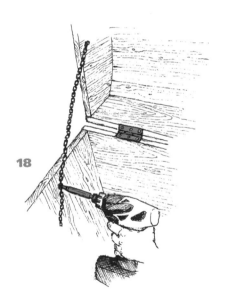

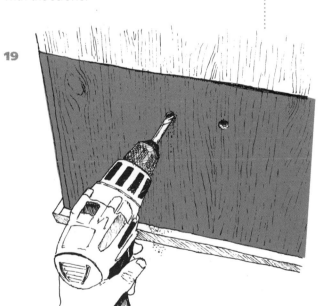

18 To stop the heavy lid from dropping back when opened and damaging the hinges, fit a length of chain to the inside of the top 3 in/7.5 cm in from the back of the left-hand side with a screw. Hold the lid in a balanced open position, then attach the other end of the chain in the center of the carcass with a screw.

19 To make it easier to move the storage chest around, make handles by drilling two ¾-in/2-cm holes in the two side panels, set 3 in/7.5 cm below the top edge of the opening and 4 in/10 cm apart. Thread a length of rope into each set of holes, and knot the ends inside the chest.

(A) *The slats sit closely together to follow the curve of the lid.* **(B)** *The plinth running around the base gives the chest a more substantial feel.* **(C)** *The front and back panels of the lid are formed from the front and back panels of the carcass of the chest.* **(D)** *The slats need to be all the same length to make sure of a flush finish.* **(E)** *Adjust the length of the chain while the lid is held open.* **(F)** *The pins of the butt hinges should protrude outside the chest.*

The completed treasure chest storage.

PICTURE PERFECT FRAME SHELVING

Here is a project that is sure to provide any dull wall space with a powerful visual impact. You can use the framed storage spaces to show off your favorite ornaments, seasonal decorations, or even plants. Whatever you choose to display, the effect will be to create your own little art gallery. For mine, I chose to add a blackboard panel to the frame in the center, making it handy for making notes and memos, but you can use a reclaimed message board. Alternatively, fitting a mirror into a frame can add an interesting dimension to the finished work, or keep the frame's original glass and display some artwork or a photograph.

TOOLS FOR THE JOB

Claw hammer

Tape measure and pencil

Handsaw

Protractor (optional)

Clamps

Hand drill with ³⁄₁₆-in/4-mm
and ⁵⁄₁₆-in/8-mm drill bits

Screwdriver

FOR AN EASY LIFE

Jigsaw

Cordless drill/driver

EXTRAS

Nails

Wood glue

Wood screws and
wall screws

LUMBER CUTTING LIST

Assorted picture frames

One ¼-by-46-by-50-in/
6-mm-by-117-by-127-cm
sheet of manufactured
board (for the frame's
backing board), plus
extra if making a panel
for the centerpiece frame
(optional)

Two 1-by-1½-by-8-in/
2.5-by-4-by-20-cm boards
(for the sides of miter box;
optional)

One 8-in 1×4/2.5-by-10-by-
20-cm board (for the
bottom of the miter box;
optional)

Assorted lengths of wood
molding or boards (to
make your own frames;
optional)

Assorted lengths of ½-by-
2½-in/1-by-6-cm boards
(for the frame boxes)

CHOOSING YOUR MATERIALS

Before starting this project, I made a few trips to garage sales and flea markets over several weekends and, eventually, I built up a good collection of picture frames in different sizes. This project works best with one large frame as the centerpiece, both visually and to support the weight of the final project when it is hung on a wall. Once I found a large picture frame that I liked, I chose the smaller frames simply because I liked how they worked with the large frame. A random symmetry produces the best results. As long as the structure of the picture frames was sturdy, the condition of the finish wasn't important because I planned to paint the frames. However, for your project, you can leave the frames in their natural, stressed patina, stain some and paint others, or paint each frame in a different bold color—whichever approach you choose, the results will be striking.

If you are short a picture frame or two, or can't find a picture frame in the size you want, you can make your own frames, using either a length of wood molding, which are made in an array of interesting profile shapes, or any square or rectangular boards you have on hand.

To build the boxes behind the frames, ideally, you will need a source of planed wood about ½ in/1 cm thick. I found a collection of old wine boxes that were ideal for this, because the wood was light enough not to add too much weight to the finished project. I knocked the boxes apart and cut the lumber down to uniform strips 2½ in/6 cm wide, which should be wide enough to support small, lightweight objects. The only other material you'll need is a thin sheet of hardboard or other manufactured board for the backing board and as a panel for the large centerpiece frame. I painted it with blackboard paint, but you can paint it an interesting color, if you prefer.

Steps

1 Remove any pictures, backing boards, glass, and nails from your frame collection, using the claw hammer. If you decide to make one of your frames a blackboard, put the frame on ¼-in/ 6-mm manufactured board, trace around it with the pencil, and cut to size with a handsaw. Secure it into place with small nails secured around the board's edge and into the frame.

2 If you have enough reclaimed picture frames, move on to step 6; if you don't, it's simple to make your own frames. To do this, first make a miter box (if you don't already have one). Glue or nail two 1-by-1½-by-8-in/ 2.5-by-4-by-20-cm boards (the sides) along the long edges of an 8-in 1×4/ 2.5-by-10-by-20-cm board, which will be the bottom of the miter box.

ASSEMBLY GUIDE

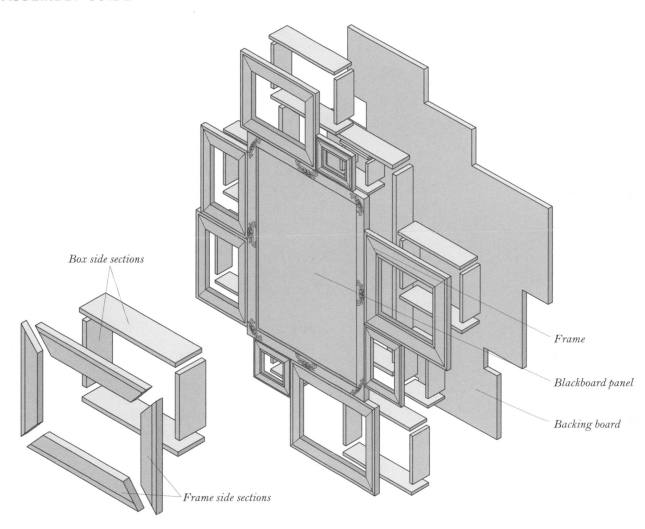

Box side sections

Frame side sections

Frame

Blackboard panel

Backing board

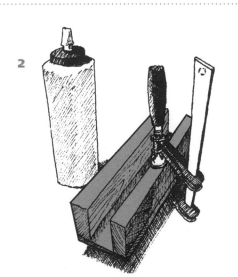

2

3 When the glue is dry, using either the protractor or the 45-degree position marked on your handsaw, mark two opposing 45-degree angles 2 in/5 cm apart. Using the handsaw, cut these angles down to the bottom board, making sure that the vertical cut lines are completely straight.

Continued

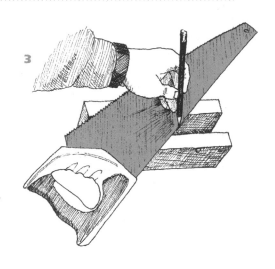

3

TIPS

- **STEP 4** When making a miter joint, it's easy to make the cut in the wrong direction; to avoid mistakes, measure and mark the cuts on the wood, then measure a second time to make sure that once the wood is cut, it won't be too short.

- **STEP 5** It can help if you either clamp or ask for an extra pair of hands to hold the frame sides as you glue and nail them together.

- **STEP 9** When cutting sheets of manufactured board with the jigsaw, always make sure the piece is properly secured in place.

When cutting sheets of manufactured wood, always wear a good-quality dust mask and eye protection.

4 Now, it's a simple task of sliding the wood for the frame into your new miter box, and cutting the miter angles on each end to your desired frame length. Be careful when making the cuts that the angles are facing the correct way so they make a 90-degree right angle when assembled (see step 5).

5 With the four frame sides cut, add a dab of wood glue to each mitered face, and tap a small nail into one side to secure the joint while the glue dries.

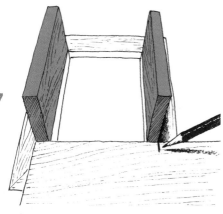

6 To make the sides around the frame openings, lay a frame facedown on the workbench, and mark the length of the opening of the frame onto one of the ½-in-/1-cm-thick boards. Cut it to size with the handsaw, and then repeat for the opposite side. Add a line of wood glue to one edge of both pieces and position them on top of the frame. Using the claw hammer and small nails, nail through the front of the frame into the box side sections.

7 Turn the frame back on its face and mark the other two side sections against the sections you have just fitted; these should overlap. Cut the last two side sections with the handsaw, then nail them into place as in step 6, and secure the butting ends with two nails.

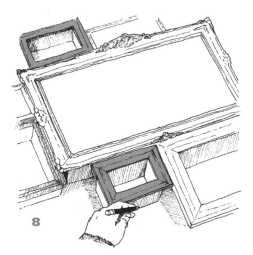

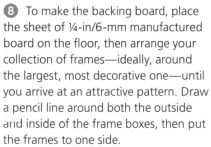

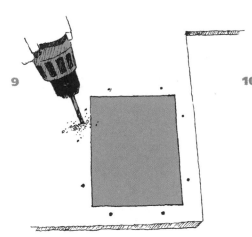

⑧ To make the backing board, place the sheet of ¼-in/6-mm manufactured board on the floor, then arrange your collection of frames—ideally, around the largest, most decorative one—until you arrive at an attractive pattern. Draw a pencil line around both the outside and inside of the frame boxes, then put the frames to one side.

⑨ Following the outside line, cut around the pattern of the frame boxes, using either the handsaw or jigsaw. After cutting, using the hand drill and ³⁄₁₆-in/4-mm drill bit, drill two holes in the board for each box side section, making sure that they are centered where the ½-in/1-cm edges will sit.

⑩ Starting with the large frame in the center, attach each frame, one at a time, to the backing board, using the screwdriver and small wood screws.

⑪ To make a simple, discreet wall fitting on the back of the board, start from the top of the large frame in the center and measure 4 in/10 cm down on each side and make a pencil mark; draw a horizontal pencil line between the two marks. Then measure and mark 3 in/7.5 cm in from the sides of the same frame along the pencil line. Now make an upside-down keyhole shape at each of these two points: first drill a ⁵⁄₁₆-in/8-mm hole, then drill two ³⁄₁₆-in/4-mm holes above each of the larger holes, but so all three holes are overlapping, and the smaller holes are closer to the top of the frame. When corresponding wall screws are secured in place, the heads of these screws will slide through the larger holes and then lock behind the smaller ones.

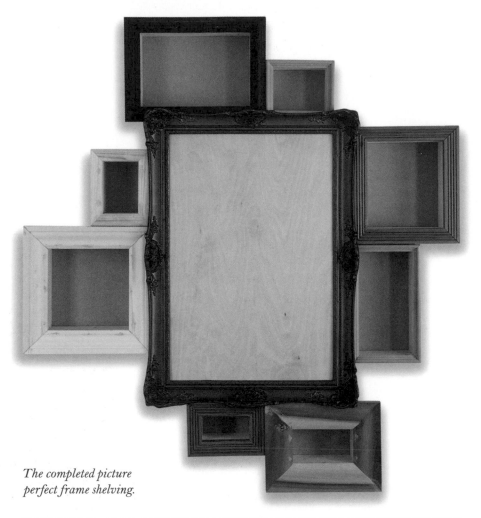

The completed picture perfect frame shelving.

(A) The keyhole-shape holes are ideal for hanging the project on a wall. (B) Painting all the picture frames gray helps them stand out against the blackboard. (C) The juxtaposition of old frames against new creates a refreshing look. (D) As long as the wood is sturdy, marks and scuffs are part of the charm of reclaimed frames.

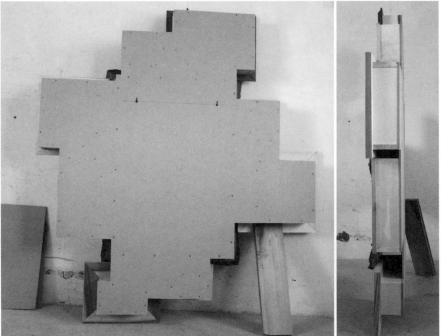

MAGIC STORAGE TABLE

There are two great reasons to make this next project. First, it is an attractive, well-proportioned table that has a variety of uses, from sitting around it with friends and a pot of coffee or a board game to using it as a working surface, whether it be for sewing or other craft projects. Second, lift the lid and you will find a large volume of storage space, which is always welcome.

TOOLS FOR THE JOB

Hand drill with ¼-in/6-mm, ³⁄₁₆-in/4-mm, and ⅜-in/ 10-mm drill bits

Tape measure and 2 pencils

Claw hammer

Clamps

Jigsaw

Surform plane or wood rasp

Sandpaper, 80- and 120-grit, and woodblock

Flat-head screwdriver

Handsaw

Straightedge

FOR AN EASY LIFE

Electric sander

Cordless drill/driver

EXTRAS

Nails

Wood screws

Wood glue

Two 4-in/10-cm strap hinges

LUMBER CUTTING LIST

One ½-by-1-by-21¾-in/ 1-by-2.5-by-55-cm board (for the trammel bar)

Two ¾-by-32½-by-32½-in/ 2-by-83-by-83-cm sheets of plywood (for the carcass top and bottom)

Thirty-four ¾-by-3-by-16-in/2-by-7.5-by-40-cm boards (for the side panels)

Four 8-in 2×2/5-by-5-by-20-cm boards (for the feet)

One ¾-by-36-by-36-in/2-by-91-by-91-cm sheet of OSB (for the tabletop)

CHOOSING YOUR MATERIALS

When you prepare your shopping list for this project, you will need three sheets of manufactured board big enough to get the diameter of table you need; two sheets are for the top and bottom of the table's carcass, and there is also a separate tabletop. You can make the table to whatever size suits your space. In order to maximize storage space, I made my table 16 in/40 cm high with a diameter of 36 in/90 cm. I reclaimed a sheet of ¾-in/2-cm oriented strand board (OSB) for the tabletop. I think the pattern of wood chip in the board adds some interest to the tabletop, but you can also use particleboard, fiberboard, or plywood. I also used two sheets of ¾-in/2-cm exterior-grade plywood for the top and bottom of the carcass, which were a 32½-in/83-cm diameter to allow for the width of the side panels—which at ¾ in/2 cm each meant subtracting 1½ in/4 cm from the tabletop—plus a 2-in/5-cm overhang.

Along with the sheet materials, you will need solid lumber boards to run around the table's side. There are two points to consider when selecting them. They should be no less than ¾ in/2 cm in thickness, because they will form the table's structure and, therefore, need to be strong. And they also need to be of a width that can sit comfortably around the table's curved boards, making as much contact as possible. For example, on my 36-in-/90-cm-diameter table, I used lengths of 3-in-/7.5-cm-wide tongue-and-groove boards reclaimed from old wall paneling. Wider boards won't rest as neatly against the curves. The only other wood you'll need are some scrap boards at least 2 in/5 cm thick for the feet.

To get the tabletop to flap open, I used a pair of 4-in/10-cm hinges. Strap hinges add a nice detail to the top, and are easy to fit, but you can use other hinges you happen to find. Depending on the style of the hinge, you may need to use an extra hinge or two to provide enough strength.

Steps

1 To mark the circle for the top of the carcass, you'll need to make a trammel (also known as a beam compass) from a wood batten that's at least 3 in/7.5 cm longer than half the diameter you intend your tabletop to be. Drill a hole into one end, using the ¼-in/6-mm drill bit, and push a pencil into the hole. To calculate the radius of the carcass top, halve the tabletop's diameter, then subtract the thickness of the boards you will use for the side (I used ¾-in-/2-cm-thick boards) and an additional 1 in/2.5 cm for the overhang. Using the tape measure and the other pencil, measure and mark from the tip of the pencil the radius you have just calculated, then use the claw hammer to tap in a nail at this point.

ASSEMBLY GUIDE

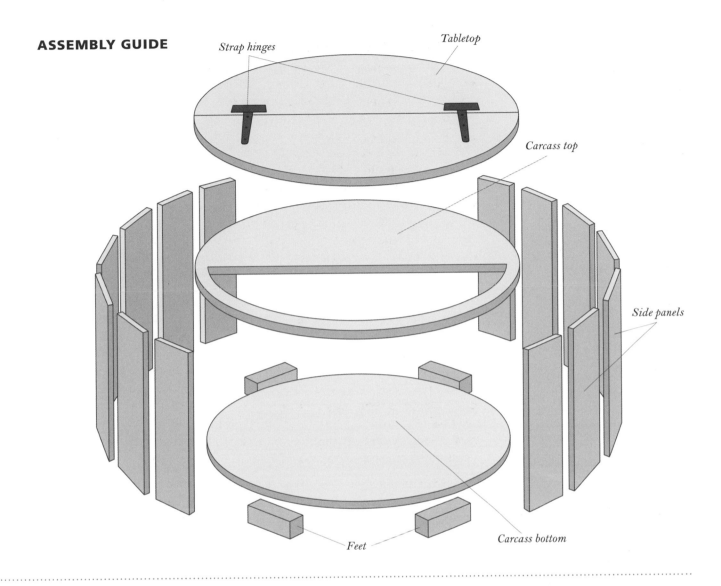

Strap hinges

Tabletop

Carcass top

Side panels

Feet

Carcass bottom

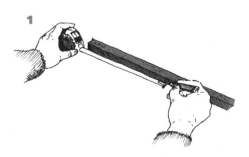

1

2 Tap the trammel nail into the center of the board for the carcass top and scribe a circle with the pencil end. Repeat again in the board for the carcass bottom, so you have two circles for the table carcass (the tabletop will be measured and marked later on, so don't throw that trammel away).

Continued

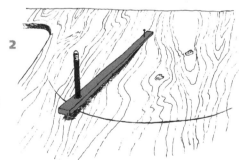

2

- **STEP 3** When operating a jigsaw, remember to keep fingers and cord away from the blade. Always wear safety goggles and a good-quality dust mask.

- **STEP 5** To ensure the disks match up, when marking the line, make one line for the first mark, two for the second, three for the third, and four for the fourth.

- **STEP 6** To work out the quantity of side panels needed, make a pencil mark on the edge of the disk, then take one board of the correct width and, working around the edge of the disk, count how many boards will fit until you return to the pencil mark. This will also help determine the ideal width of the boards.

If the boards you have for the side panels don't fit evenly around the disks, work out the gap that will be left over, and divide it into either two or four. Cut some boards to this width, and space them evenly around the table, two at opposite ends or four every fourth of the table. This will look neater than having all the additional boards together, and they can provide an interesting contrast if you use a different type of wood.

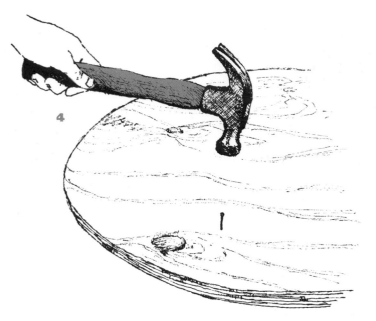

3 Clamp the two boards safely to a stable working surface. Following the pencil lines of the scribed circles, cut out both the carcass top and bottom disks, using the jigsaw.

4 Stack together the two disks, aligning the edges as much as possible, then temporarily secure them together by tapping in two nails. (This will help keep the edges of the disks identical as you remove any bumps left by the jigsaw.) Use the Surform plane or wood rasp to remove any bumps and smooth the edges. Finish off the edges, first with 80-grit sandpaper, then with 120-grit paper until the edges are smooth.

5 When cleaned up, mark four pencil lines spaced evenly along the edges of the two disks—these will be reference points when you fit the side panels on them. Using a flat-head screwdriver, pry apart the disks. Remove the nails using the claw hammer.

6 Decide on the height you want your table to be, then subtract the thickness of the tabletop and the feet. Use this measurement to mark one of the 3-in/ 7.5-cm boards you have for the table's side panels. Using the handsaw, cut it to length, then write "template" on it. Use the template to cut the remainder of the side panels.

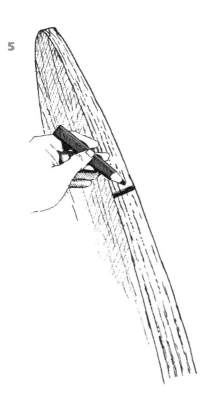

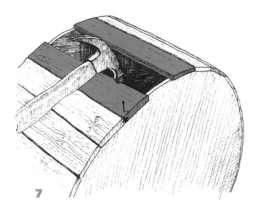

7

8

7 Stand both the top and bottom disks on their edges—having an extra pair of hands or clamping one disk to a bench will help. Use the pencil marks made on the edges to keep the disks—and any sanding irregularities—aligned. Now, start nailing the side panels in place. The ends of the panels should be flush with the face of both the top and bottom disks. If necessary, trim the last side panel to fit, using the handsaw.

8 The table will need some feet to keep it off the floor, so turn it upside-down onto its top. Drill two pilot holes in each of four 8-in 2×2/5-by-5-by-20-cm boards, using the 3/16-in/4-mm drill bit. The feet are not a feature of the table, so set them in from the edge about 3 in/7.5 cm and secure them in place with wood screws. Now turn the table upright on its feet.

TIPS

- **STEP 7** Do you find a lot of the nails you hammer in are bending? Try rubbing the face of your hammer onto a piece of sandpaper placed on a flat surface. A shiny face on the hammer will help the nails go in straight because the hammer will strike the nail evenly—a rusty or pitted face may deflect the nail's head when it is struck.

- **STEP 9** If you don't have a straightedge for marking the centerline, a straight length of wood board will do, as long as it's long enough to go across the tabletop.

9 It's now time to make an access hole to get to the storage area. Using the tape measure, find the center of the carcass top, then with the pencil and the straightedge, draw a line along the center of the top. Grab your trammel and move the nail from its original position to 3 in/7.5 cm closer to the pencil at the other end. Position the nail at the center of the line drawn on the carcass top, tap it in place with the hammer, then scribe a semicircle. It should be 3 in/7.5 cm in from the top's edge, not including the side panels.

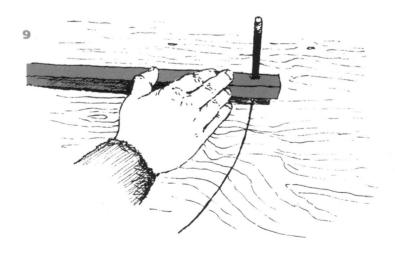

9

Continued

- **STEP 10** Before placing the jigsaw into the drill hole, make sure that the power is off. The blade should be able to sit in the hole without contacting the wood, so that it will not snatch when switched on.

When using the jigsaw, always wear safety goggles and a good-quality dust mask.

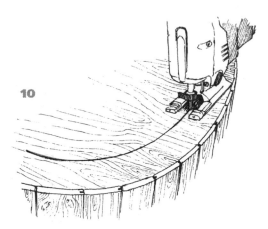

10 With the semicircle shape drawn out on the carcass top, make a hole into it, using the ⅜-in/10-mm drill bit. Insert the blade of the jigsaw into the hole, then follow the pencil lines to remove the shape. Using 120-grit sandpaper, clean up the cutout edge, paying attention to sharp corners—you don't want people getting splinters as they store their stuff in the table.

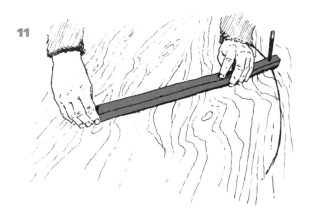

11 I hope you still have that trammel, because you will need it one last time. Measure from the nail in the opposite direction of the pencil by 4 in/10 cm, plus the thickness of the material used for the side panels. Reposition the nail at this point. Now, mark out the circle for the tabletop on the sheet of board you have set aside. This will give your tabletop a 1-in/2.5-cm overhang from the carcass.

12 Before cutting out the circle, using the straightedge, draw a pencil line through the center of the circle—you can use the hole left by the trammel nail as a reference point. Securing the top to your work surface with the clamp, cut out the circle with the jigsaw, then cut it in half through the centerline with the handsaw. Give the top faces and edges a good sanding with 120-grit sandpaper, paying particular attention to remove any sharp edges.

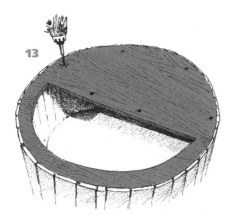

- **STEP 14** Keep the glue spread about 1-in/2.5-cm in from the edge of the carcass top. This will help prevent the glue from being squeezed out and making a mess when the tabletop is fitted. If, despite this precaution, some does escape, simply wipe it away with a damp cloth before it cures.

- **STEP 15** All that remains to do is decide on a finish you think will suit both the table and the space you want to place it in. Whether you apply a coat of paint, color stain, or clear finish, this table works with them all.

⓭ Back on the table carcass, drill about six ³⁄₁₆-in/4-mm pilot holes into the half of the carcass top that was not cut out. Position them so that there are four spaced evenly around and about 2 in/5 cm away from the curved edges and two spaced evenly along and about 2 in/5 cm away from the straight edge at the center of the top.

⓮ Evenly spread wood glue over the solid half of the carcass top, then fit one half of the tabletop over the carcass, checking that it has its 1-in/2.5-cm overhang around the edge. When the tabletop is in place, secure it from inside the carcass with the wood screws.

⓯ Position the free half of the tabletop in place next to the fastened half, leaving a ³⁄₁₆-in/4-mm gap between the two to prevent the top from binding when opening. Position the two strap hinges about 3 in/7.5 cm in from each end and screw in place. The top should now flip back freely.

The completed magic storage table.

(A) *When closed, the tabletop covers the edges of the side panels, providing a neat finish.* **(B)** *Fit the side panels as closely together as you can.* **(C)** *When positioning the hinges, allow a gap so the top can open and close smoothly.* **(D)** *For a natural finish, before nailing the side panels in place, arrange them based on their color and wood grain.*

THE LOG STORE

Let's face it, on a cold winter night with a strong wind and the snow falling in abundance, the last thing you want to do is trek through that snow to get logs for the fire. This log store is quick and easy to build and looks handsome enough to grace any front porch or backyard. The design of the store allows for air to flow around the stack, drying the logs and helping to prevent the start of rot or any fungal growth. And what's more, its traditional shingle roof will help keep your logs dry and ready for the fire.

TOOLS FOR THE JOB
Tape measure and pencil

Piece of paper

Clamp or vise

Handsaw

Claw hammer

Screwdriver

FOR AN EASY LIFE
Cordless drill/driver

Jigsaw or round

Surform plane

EXTRAS
Nails and wood screws

LUMBER CUTTING LIST
One 20½-by-27½-in/52-by-70-cm pallet (for the base)

Thirty 4-by-20½-in/10-by-52-cm fence posts (for the side pieces)

Two 4-by-11-in/10-by-28-cm scraps (to support the roof joint)

Four 1-by-3-by-60-in/2.5-by-7.5-by-150-cm boards (for the side posts)

Four 1-by-5-by-30-in/2.5-by-12-by-76-cm boards (for the back pieces)

Two ¾-by-24-by-24-in/2-by-61-by-61-cm sheets of manufactured board (for the roof panels)

Enough ½-by-4-in/1-by-10-cm boards to cut 120 (4-in/10-cm) squares (for the roof shingles)

Two ¾-by-4-by-28-in/2-by-10-by-71-cm boards (for the roof fascia)

CHOOSING YOUR MATERIALS

All the wooden parts needed to make up the store are easy to find. Its style can be altered to suit your own tastes or adapted to tie in with the look of your house. The log store is built around a pallet, so the size is dictated by the size of pallet you use. If you place the pallet where you'll want to keep your log store, you'll have a better idea of the dimensions that will work with its surroundings. Check that there are no obstructions or other issues, such as the store blocking house doors from opening. If your need for logs is greater than for most homes with a fireplace, you can increase the size of the log store by using two pallets of the same size.

For the store's side sections, I decided to use some reclaimed semicircular fence posts I had on hand. I felt the look of the end-grain shape of the fence posts would give the project a real "woody" feel. If fence posts such as these are hard to find, half-logs or any type of wooden boards will be fine. Old floorboards were more than adequate for the four back pieces, and they would also be suitable for the side pieces, if you prefer.

For the roof of this project, any exterior-grade manufactured board will be fine, but a thickness of ¾ in/2 cm is best to provide strength without adding too much weight. The great thing about a wooden shingle roof is the more random the shingles, or tiles, the more rustic and attractive the result. I acquired a pickup-truck load of fruit boxes from a local produce market. These are made from thin, rough-cut softwood that is ideal for roof shingles when the boxes are disassembled. For the 120 shingles used in my store, I needed 40 ft/12 m of wood, but that doesn't include the waste from making the cuts. You should calculate an extra ¼ in/6 mm for each cut—and the fact that you'll probably have plenty of short leftover scrap ends as wastage.

Steps

1 With the pallet in its final position, use the tape measure to establish its width and depth, then measure to get an idea of the finished height you want the store to be. Roughly sketch out the shape of the log store on the piece of paper, adding the measurements.

2 Armed with your sketch and measurements, it's time to start cutting some lumber. Secure a fence post or board with a clamp. Using the handsaw, cut the wood to the depth of the pallet (from front to back). Repeat until you have enough pieces to fit the side sections for the desired height. If, for example, the final height of the side sections will be 5 ft/1.5 m and your fence posts are 4 in/10 cm wide, you'll need 15 fence posts per side.

ASSEMBLY GUIDE

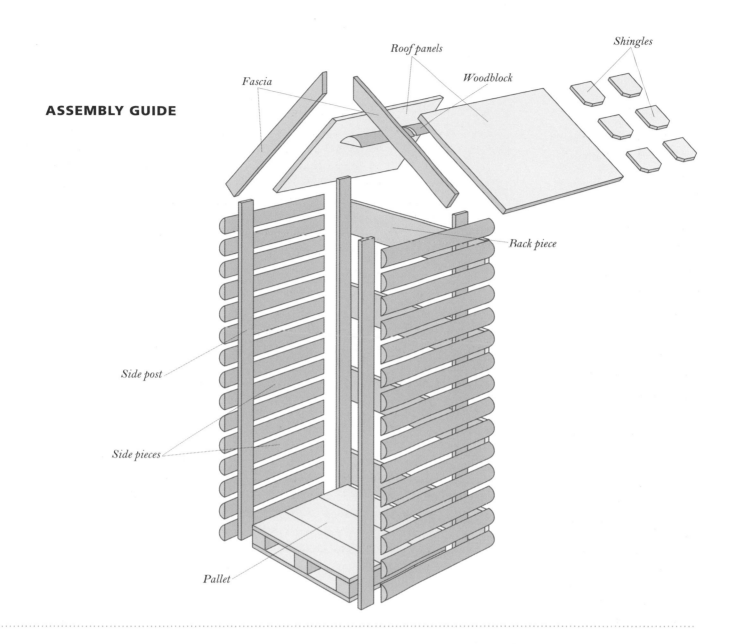

Fascia

Roof panels

Woodblock

Shingles

Back piece

Side post

Side pieces

Pallet

③ Next, you will need four 1-by-3-in/ 2.5-by-7.5-cm boards for the side posts. Cut them to the height you want the sides to be. Lay out the side pieces (in my case, the fence posts) for one side section on the floor, exterior-side facing down. Place one 1-by-3-in/2.5-by-7.5-cm side post along each edge of the side pieces; then nail or screw through the side posts into each side piece.

Continued

TIP

- **STEP 3** Don't worry if the side pieces have gaps between them; the gaps will help the flow of air.

- **STEP 4** Fitting large wood screws is made easier if you predrill one of the components first with a ³⁄₁₆-in/4-mm drill bit.

  Before using the screws, run them through a wax candle so the wax in the screw threads will make it easier to drive them in.

- **STEP 6** If you feel creating a pitched roof would be too challenging, a flat roof will work just as well. Use the measurements of the pallet as a guide for size, adding 3 in/7.5 cm all around to provide for an overhang.

- **STEP 10** For an alternative look, use a Surform plane to round off the exposed edge of the shingles instead of trimming the corners.

- **STEP 11** If you have a budding woodworker around, this is a fantastic opportunity to get him or her involved. It's a simple and safe task that will provide a youngster with a great sense of achievement.

- **STEP 13** To add some character, I split an old axe handle in half and nailed it to the fascia.

4 This step is a lot easier if you have a buddy on hand. Position the two side sections on the floor, with the pallet between them and flush at the bottom edges. Using the biggest wood screws you can—but make sure that they are not so long they will break through the other side—secure the bottom of the side sections to the pallet with screws.

5 Without moving the components of the frame, use the tape measure to check that the width between the top of the side sections is the same as the width across the bottom, where the pallet is fitted. Using wood screws or nails, secure a back piece flush to the top of the side sections, then the bottom. To make the log store rigid and sturdy, secure at least two more back pieces evenly between the two side sections.

6 Now for the pitched roof. First grab a couple of boards from your scrap pile. With the frame still facing down on the floor, lay the scrap boards at the top at about a 90-degree angle, with the ends at the peak butting together and a little overhang at the sides. Measure the length of the boards with the tape measure and note the measurements on the sketch. Measure the depth of the log store and add 3 in/7.5 cm. With these measurements, you now have the size for the two panels to make the roof.

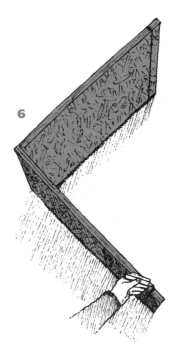

7 With a pencil and tape measure, mark the measurements on the manufactured boards and secure them with a clamp. Cut the panels to size with the handsaw.

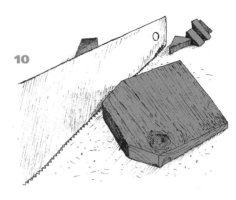

8 Position the panels, laying them against the top of the store frame to check the fit; then secure them along the top edge, at the roof's peak, with screws or nails. For added strength, use two scraps from the side pieces as woodblocks, securing them into the underside of the roof panels.

9 Time to call on that buddy again to lift the log store frame the right way up. Now line up the roof and set it flush with the back of the frame. When you are satisfied with its position, secure the roof in place by driving long wood screws through the roof into the frame.

10 For the shingles, cut the softwood into 4-in/10-cm squares, using the handsaw and with the work secured in a clamp. To add some detail, cut off the two exposed corners with the handsaw.

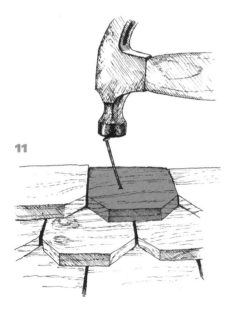

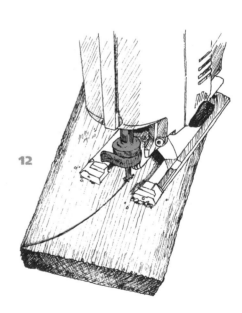

12 With the shingles in place, the final task is to add the fascia to the front of the log store to give your roof a more professional look. You'll need two boards equal to the length of the side panels, and these will need to be mitered at a 45-degree angle so the ends butt together at the peak of the roof. Use a triangle to measure the angle if you don't have a miter box (or see page 143). If you want, shape the bottom corner edges of the fascia, using either a jigsaw or a round Surform plane.

11 When you feel you have enough shingles with a few spares for mishaps, start to nail them into place with the claw hammer and 1-in/2.5-cm nails. Start at the bottom of the roof and work up, working on one horizontal row at a time. On each new row, center the shingle over the joint of the two lower ones. This will create a striking pattern—and remember a little rustic unevenness is a good thing.

13 Check the fit of the fascia pieces before securing them to the log store, making sure you are satisfied with how they butt together. Then simply nail or screw them into place.

The completed log store.

(A) *Semicircular fence posts make excellent side pieces, but so will split logs or old floorboards.* **(B)** *Whether you use fence posts or other pieces of scrap wood, woodblocks give the roof extra stability.* **(C)** *You may have enough material from a single source for a roof in a solid color or* tone, but you can also mix up different materials to create an interesting random look. **(D)** *Staggering the joints in the rows of overlapping shingles helps provide a watertight roof.* **(E)** *Weathered, stained wood adds interest to the fascia, but you can add a fresh stain, if you prefer.*

THE SLATTY CHAIR

Letting people know that you are in the market for any old wood can pay off. A neighbor once asked me if I had any use for the two old and outgrown children's beds she was about to throw out. She was obviously embarrassed to offer them to me, but while she saw them as junk, I could envision the relaxing porch chair I had been promising myself.

This project is easy to put together, yet it looks great when finished and gets plenty of admiring comments from family and friends—a boost to the confidence of any budding woodworker.

TOOLS FOR THE JOB

Tape measure and pencil

Black felt-tip marking pen

Jigsaw

Clamp or vise

Handsaw

Claw hammer

Sandpaper, 80-grit, and woodblock

Hand drill with ³/₁₆-in/4-mm drill bit

Screwdriver

FOR AN EASY LIFE

Wood rasp

Cordless drill/driver

EXTRAS

Wood glue

Nails

Wood screws

LUMBER CUTTING LIST

Two ¾-by-39½-by-39½-in/ 2-by-100-by-100-cm sheets of manufactured board (for the two side sections)

Seventy ¾-by-1½-by-31½-in/ 2-by-4-by-80-cm boards (for the slats), plus 5-in-/ 12-cm-long scraps (for the woodblocks)

Two 31½-in 1x6/2.5-by-15-by-80-cm boards (for the bracing rails)

Two ¾-by-1½-by-6-in/ 2-by-4-by-15-cm boards (for the battens)

CHOOSING YOUR MATERIALS

I was lucky because the bed slats were the perfect size for my chair, being ¾ by 2 in/2 by 5 cm, which is close enough to the size of standard 1×2/2.5 by 5 cm boards. If you are using recycled softwood boards instead of bed slats, use 1x2/2.5 by 5 cm boards. (This is their "nominal" size, the size they were before being planed at the mill; their actual size is ¾ by 1½ in/ 2 by 4 cm.) If the only slats or boards you have are wider, ask someone at your local lumberyard to rip them down for you. Getting on the good side of the people at the lumberyard can be helpful when you need lumber cut to size, wood scraps, or just some professional advice.

For my chair sides, I used oriented strand board (OSB); however, any type of manufactured board will work, although one that is durable outdoors is preferable. I decided to finish the board with a matte black exterior paint because I thought it would create a powerful visual effect and act as a strong contrast to the wood slats. However, you can keep the manufactured board in its natural state, which looks great, too, or paint it a more subtle color. You can also apply a wood stain to the slats.

Getting a comfortable chair shape is probably the greatest challenge in this project. Measure other chairs you have around or a friend's chair to use as reference measurements for your chair; you'll be surprised at just how low the seat on this type of chair has to be. You should measure the height of the seat from the floor, the depth and width of the seat, and the height of the backrest from the floor and from the seat. Make sure you make the chair deep enough from front to back at ground level, with the backrest not too steeply angled backward, to prevent the chair from tipping back as you recline with your iced drink.

Steps

1 With your measurements on hand and a thick pencil, mark out on the manufactured board a curved shape that will give you the side profile for your chair, following the photograph on page 166. Once you are satisfied with the outline, go around it with a black marking pen to make it easier to see when cutting.

2 Because of the side's curved shape, the jigsaw is essential. With the board securely held with the clamp, cut along the marked line with the jigsaw. The more you can stay on the line, the less cleanup time there will be, and you'll have a neater result.

ASSEMBLY GUIDE

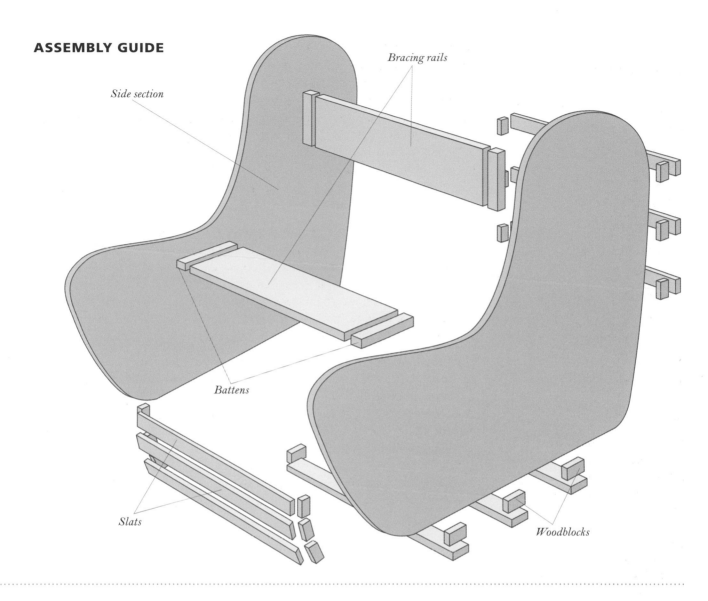

Side section

Bracing rails

Battens

Slats

Woodblocks

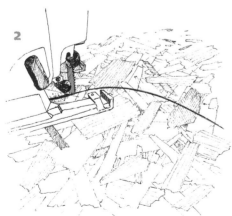

2

3 Use the cutout side section as a template to mark out the other side section, and saw it in the same way as in step 2.

3

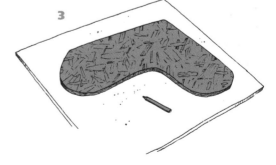

Continued

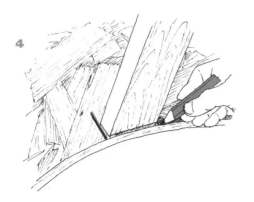

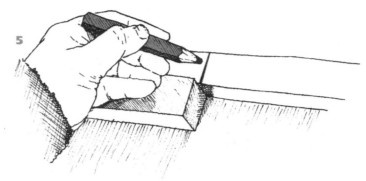

④ To do a rough count of the slats required, place a slat on the edge of one of the side sections and make pencil marks on each side. Move the slat over, aligning it so only one edge is at a pencil mark, then make another pencil mark at the opposite side. Continue marking around the side section until you return to the first pencil mark. You may need to adjust the spacing so there are no gaps. Count the number of slats you'll need.

⑤ For my chair, I decided on a width of 32 in/81 cm; however, depending on the space you have for the chair, and the wood you have for your slats, you can adjust this measurement (but don't make it so wide that it will sag in the middle). Using a tape measure, mark the length you want on one of the slats and cut it with the handsaw. Use this measured piece as a guide to cut the rest of the slats. This method will prevent any misreading of the tape measure, which can lead to slats in many sizes, none of which you'll want. You should be left with a pile of scraps, which you'll need for the next step.

⑥ The only downside to using any manufactured board material is its poor ability to take nails or screws along its edge. If you try driving a screw into the edge of the board, it will cause the board to split and the joint will be weak. However, there is a solution: make woodblocks from scrap wood and attach them to the internal faces of the two side sections. First, you'll need to measure and cut short lengths from the leftover scraps of slats so they fit around the curve of the side sections. You may need to angle some of the cuts to help them fit together.

⑦ Attach the woodblocks on the inside surface of the side sections, following the curved edge, using wood glue and a few nails, and let the glue dry. Don't worry if they stick out in places beyond the curves. Once the glue dries, trim off any protruding areas with the jigsaw.

⑧ Run your eye around the edge of the side sections, looking for any unsightly bumps. Remove them with 80-grit sandpaper wrapped around a woodblock (or use a wood rasp, if you have one).

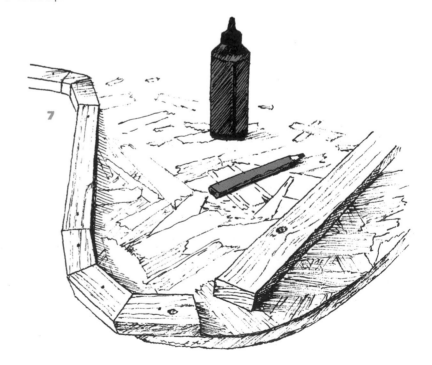

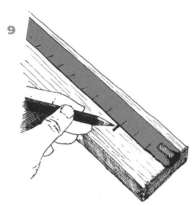

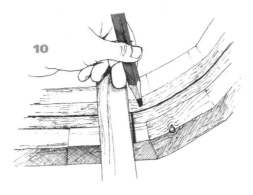

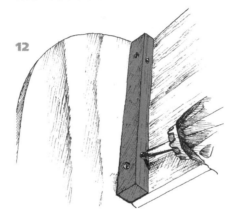

⑨ On a prepared slat, measure in from one end 1¼ in/3 cm, and mark with a pencil. Use the marked slat as a guide to mark the rest. Make pilot holes at the pencil marks, using a ³⁄₁₆-in/4-mm drill bit. These will be screw holes for assembly. Apply any finish or paint to the slats and side sections; let them dry.

⑩ To get the sides to line up, place them side by side so that the exterior sides are together and the edges are aligned. Mark two clear lines across the edges. Turn the pieces around so the interiors are facing each other, and temporarily attach two slats on these lines, using screws; these will hold the sides parallel while you assemble the chair.

⑪ For extra strength, make two bracing rails by cutting two 1x6/2.5-by-15-cm boards to the length of the slats minus the thickness of the two side sections, using the handsaw, and cut four battens from ¾-by-1½-in/2-by-4-cm boards to 6 in/15 cm long. Use the drill bit to make pilot holes into the battens, two on each end, on adjacent faces and slightly staggered so the screws don't go into each other. Screw the battens flush to the ends of the bracing rails.

⑫ Position one of the bracing rails between the two side sections, inside the batten edge, near the knee area, and drive a screw through each pilot hole in the battens. Repeat with the other bracing rail near the head area. Remove the temporary slats.

⑬ Secure the permanent slats into place using screws, going through the pilot holes and into the woodblocks along the inside edge of the side sections. The screws should be long enough to go about halfway through the woodblocks.

TIPS

- **STEP 8** When cutting with any power tool, make sure the workpiece is situated on a stable, flat surface. Use clamps or a vise to hold it securely, or ask somebody to steady the board for you.

  When operating a jigsaw, be aware of your fingers and the electrical cord in relation to the blade.

  When working with manufactured board, always wear goggles and a dust mask.

- **STEP 9** Place a piece of scrap wood under the slat when drilling to help prevent the wood from splitting on the other side of the work.

- **STEP 10** Finish the slats in an exterior wood stain, and the side panels in the chosen color prior to securing them in place. It makes the finishing job much easier.

The completed slatty chair.

(A) *Try to keep the spacing between the slats as even as possible, and aim to keep the gaps small.* **(B)** *Keep the edges of the slats aligned for a neat finish.* **(C)** *If you prefer the chair to have a natural finish, arrange the slats so that the color and grain are balanced.* **(D)** *Because the slats go around a tight curve, adjust them so that the gaps between them are as small as possible.*

FRIDAY–
NIGHT BAR

You can impress your friends by starting
a get-together or party with drinks served
from your own, unique bar—one that you
made yourself. A striking feature whether
you set it up indoors in a den, game room,
or converted basement, or on a deck in
your yard, this bar will be practical as well
as the centerpiece of the party. Don't let
the scale of this project intimidate you—it
may be large, but it's easy to put together.

TOOLS FOR THE JOB

Flat-head screwdriver

Sandpaper, 80- and
120-grit, and woodblock

Tape measure, pencil,
straightedge, and string

Jigsaw

Handsaw

Wood rasp

Hand drill with ³⁄₁₆-in/4-mm
drill bit

FOR AN EASY LIFE

Cordless drill/driver

Electric sander

EXTRAS

Nails and wood screws

LUMBER CUTTING LIST

One 2-by-15½-by-59-in/
5-by-39-by-150-cm board
(for the top)

Two ¾-by-17½-by-55-in/
2-by-45-by-140-cm sheets
of manufactured board
(for the base section
and shelf)

Two ¾-by-15-by-33¼-in/
2-by-38-by-84-cm sheets
of manufactured board
(for the side sections)

Two 4¾-by-33¼-in/12-by-
84-cm semicircular fence
posts (for the front posts)

14 ft/4.2 m of 1¼-in/3-cm
board (for the battens)

Five 2-by-10-in/5-by-25-cm
semicircular fence posts
(for the feet; rough
measurements, depending
on available scraps)

Twenty-nine 25-in 1×2/
2.5-by-5-by-64-cm boards
(for the front section)

CHOOSING YOUR MATERIALS

I came across the solid wood for the top at a lumberyard, where, because of its curved nature, it had been discarded and left in the reject pile. As an alternative to this lucky find, I could have used either a suitable sheet of manufactured board, which can be cut to a satisfactory curve, or three sections of wood cut and joined at angles to form a three-sided shape. Alternatively, the bar could simply be made with straight lines.

All of the other materials needed were easy to find. The carcass was built from a single sheet of reclaimed, marine-grade ¾-in/2-cm plywood. The front section may have a solid appearance, but in between the two semicircular fence posts, it is made up of a collection of treated, rough-sawn 1×2/2.5-by-5-cm softwood found on a construction site. I used five scrap pieces trimmed from the semicircular fence posts to make the feet.

The curve at the front of the base section and shelf is based on the shape of the wood used for the top. If the top has an exaggerated curve, tone it down as you copy it onto these pieces so the overall appearance of the frame of the bar is more subtle and it will be easier to apply the boards for the front section. The base section and shelf were made deeper than the top to provide more storage space and make the bar more sturdy. If you use a wide piece of wood for the top, you can make the base section and shelf the same depth if you want a slightly easier project or if you just prefer a more clean look with less curves. The top should be at least 15½ in/39 cm wide to prevent the bar from tipping over.

Although the other projects in this book can be created without the use of a jigsaw, we've recommended it here because it can be difficult to cut matching curves by hand. However, if you feel up to a challenge, you can try using a coping saw for making the curved cuts. Have plenty of blades on hand—you may go through a few broken ones during the project.

Steps

1 The curve of the bar will be dictated by the shape of the top, so it's best to start here and work down. To give my bar a real woody feel, I decided to leave the rough appearance on the solid wood top. For the same look, simply clean away any loose bark or dead wood from the edge, using the flat-head screwdriver, then smooth out rough edges with 80-grit sandpaper.

2 Lay down the wood top onto the sheet for the base section, and draw around the top with the pencil to act as a guide for marking out the base section. Now, for the angles and straight sides, draw straight lines on the board that follow the sides of the outline drawn around the top, using the straightedge. To smooth out the curve along the front—if you are not good at making

ASSEMBLY GUIDE

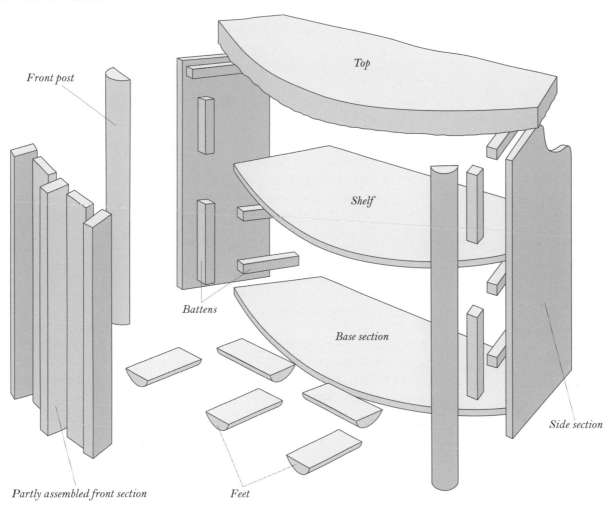

Front post

Top

Shelf

Base section

Battens

Side section

Partly assembled front section

Feet

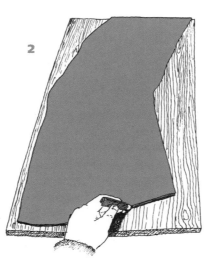

freehand curves—attach the pencil to a long piece of string, securing the other end of the string to a pivot point (such as a nail with a large head in a scrap board). The longer the piece of string, the gentler the curve. Using the tape measure and pencil, measure and mark the depth of the base section to extend it to 17½ in/ 45 cm. Using the jigsaw, cut out the base section.

Continued

2

TIP

• **STEP 1** Keep both hands behind the screwdriver when removing the bark or dead wood; it's easy to slip and injure yourself when in full flow of the job.

TIPS

- **STEP 4** When cutting sheet material, make sure the workpiece is secure and stable. Always wear safety goggles and a good-quality dust mask when using the jigsaw.

- **STEP 9** Work out from the center of the curved front to create an even spread of flat and edge boards.

- **STEP 11** If your bar has a solid wood top, it will look at its best after a good sanding. Start with 80-grit sandpaper wrapped around a block, or better still attached to an electric sander, and work in the direction of the grain. When you feel the surface is looking even, switch to a 120-grit for a smoother finish. Always wear a good-quality dust mask when sanding.

To bring together all of the wood colors used for the bar, you may want to use one of the many exterior grade protective wood stains available. If you have found a good-quality piece of lumber for the bar top, bring out all of its potential with a marine varnish, which will help protect it from the weather—and the wild party nights.

3 Use the base section as a template for the shelf and trace around it with the pencil. Because the shelf will be sitting inside the carcass, you will need to reduce its width by the thickness of the side sections. Mark in from each short end the thickness of the sheet for the side sections—in my case ¾ in/ 2 cm. Cut out the shelf, using the jigsaw.

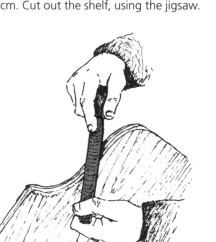

5 Make a curve on the top back corner of each side section to provide a smooth transition from the deeper shelf and base sections to the top. Using the pencil, mark a curve that starts above where you intend to fix the shelf and ends at the back edge of the top. Cut out the curve, using the jigsaw. Soften the edges with the wood rasp, then smooth them with 80-grit sandpaper.

4 Measure and mark the two side sections, using the tape measure and pencil. My top is 2 in/5 cm thick, the feet are 2 in/5 cm high, and the base section is ¾ in/2 cm thick, so I subtracted 4¾ in/12 cm from 38 in/96 cm, the height I wanted the bar to be, making my sides 33¼ in/84 cm high. Measure and mark the two fence posts to the same height, and cut them to length with the handsaw.

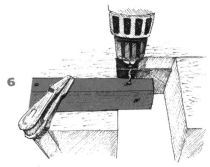

6 With the main bar components cut out, it's time to start fitting together the pieces using battens and wood screws. Using at least 1¼-in/3-cm boards, cut four battens to the width of the bar's side sections. Drill three ³⁄₁₆-in/4-mm pilot holes through each of two adjacent faces in each batten. Using the screwdriver and wood screws, attach one batten flush with the bottom edge on each side section, then measure up to the point you want the shelf to be—mine is 24 in/61 cm from the bottom—and secure the next batten here.

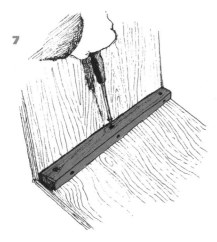

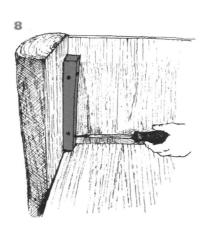

7 If you are able to get a helping hand, the next stage will be much easier. First, using the screwdriver, attach the base section to the side sections with the battens and wood screws. Now, line up the shelf and attach it to the side sections with battens and wood screws, too.

8 Measure, mark, and cut four battens to fit along the front vertical edge of the side sections, both above and below the shelf. Make pilot holes as in step 6 and secure the battens to the side sections with wood screws (but leave a gap of at least 1½ in/4 cm for the batten to attach the top). Now, use the battens to attach the fence posts, driving wood screws through the battens and into the posts.

9 To make the front section of the bar, measure the distance from the shelf to the base section and mark it on a board. Using the handsaw, cut it to size, then use this board as a template to mark and cut the rest of the boards for the front. To create the pattern on the front, start by nailing one board on its flat face to the edges of the shelf and base sections. Set the next board on its edge and nail it to the first board (not the shelf and base sections). Set the next board on its flat edge and nail it to the shelf and base sections, and repeat.

10 It's time to fit the bar top in place. With the same techniques and type of board used for the battens in step 6, measure, mark, and cut two battens, then secure them in place flush with the top of the side sections, along the inside, using wood screws. Set the top in place, and secure it by driving in wood screws through the battens from below.

11 Flip the carcass upside-down onto its top. Use scraps from the fence posts as feet for the bar. Space the five feet evenly around the bottom, with one in the center, and draw around them with a pencil. Drill two $\frac{3}{16}$-in/4-mm holes inside each of the pencil lines. After placing the feet back within the pencil marks, secure them in place with screws driven through the holes from inside the carcass and into the feet.

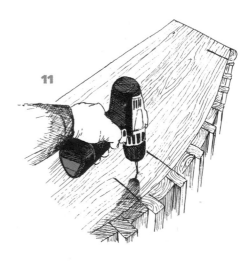

The completed
Friday-night bar.

(A) *The solid wood top still has rough edges, making it an attractive, rustic piece.* **(B)** *The front has been left in a natural finish, but you may prefer to stain alternate boards or to paint them.* **(C)** *The bar top overhangs the side sections and front posts.* **(D)** *The curves along the side sections mean sharp corners won't be a problem.* **(E)** *Half the boards forming the front section protrude, creating an interesting pattern.*

SUN LOUNGER

Whether you choose to position your lounger alongside a pool or on a deck, it's bound to provide the perfect place for relaxation on hot leisurely days. The best thing about this project has to be that, after working hard to make it, you can chill out, open a cold drink, and relax in the sun. Your only problem will be that these loungers look so inviting, you may need to make at least one more so you can keep one off-limits to everyone but yourself. Not only are they tailor-made for your comfort, but tucked at the back is a handy shelf for your book, sunscreen, and cool drink.

TOOLS FOR THE JOB

Tape measure and pencil

Piece of paper

Sandpaper, 120-grit, and woodblock

Clamps

Jigsaw

Claw hammer

Wood rasp or Surform plane

Handsaw

Hand drill and ³⁄₁₆-in/4-mm drill bit

Screwdriver

FOR AN EASY LIFE

Electric sander

Cordless drill/driver

EXTRAS

Nails

Wood screws

Wood glue

2 pairs wheels

LUMBER CUTTING LIST

One 4×8/1.2-by-2.4-m plywood sheet, minimum thickness of ¾ in/2 cm (for the side sections and frame rails)

7 ft/2.2 m of 1½-by-1½-in/ 4-by-4-cm board (for the battens)

Two 10-in 2×2/5-by-5-by-25-cm boards (for the feet)

Sixty-six 1¼-by-1½-by-26-in/3-by-4-by-66-cm boards (for the slats)

CHOOSING YOUR MATERIALS

This job is straightforward to put together and is made from basic supplies that are easily found. The two side sections and all of the frame rails were cut from one 4×8/1.2-by-2.4-m sheet of ¾-in/2-cm exterior-grade plywood discarded on a construction site. To use this one sheet for all these components, you'll need to make sure that you use the sheet wisely. When marking out the shape for the first side section, work toward one corner to make sure you leave enough material to cut out the second section and the supporting pieces; the same applies when you cut out the second side section. A jigsaw is used for this project because it is the easiest tool for cutting the curved shapes.

The top slats were retrieved from the waste pile of a local lumberyard. To them, they were useless leftovers from a production run; to me, they were the essential component to give my lounger a classic look and comfortable feel. Without the lucky break from the lumberyard, I probably would have been on the hunt for old bed-frame slats or something similar with a smooth, not rough, finish. The battens I used were cut from 1½-by-1½-in/4-by-4-cm board. You'll also need a short length of 2×2/5-by-5-cm board to make the feet at the back.

The two sets of wheels are not essential, but they will make it easier to move your lounger around to catch the most of those rays. I used old skateboard wheels, because as well as being economical and easy to find, they are good and strong and have a low profile. Wheels from an old office chair will also work.

Steps

① Make a rough sketch of the lounger to use as a working drawing; it doesn't have to be anything fancy. First, using the tape measure and pencil, record the distance from the sole of your foot to your waist and from your waist to the top of your head. Depending on how tall you are, you may wish to increase each measurement a little to allow for taller friends. Measure yourself at your widest point, whether that is your hips or shoulders, and allow a little extra for comfort. Next, throw a stack of pillows and cushions on the floor, and arrange both them and yourself into a reclined position that you would be comfortable to stay in for an hour or two. Use the measurements and the arrangement of the cushions to create a sketch of the length of the bed and the backrest.

ASSEMBLY GUIDE

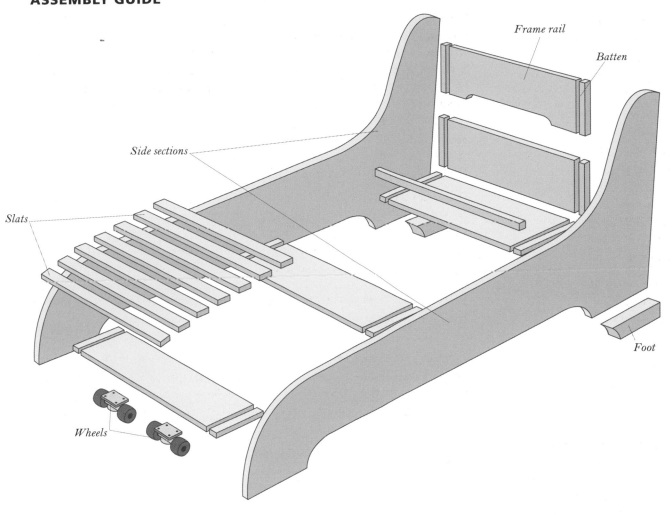

Frame rail

Batten

Side sections

Slats

Wheels

Foot

2 With sketch in hand and using the pencil, mark the shape of the side of your lounger onto the plywood. Start by measuring and marking the bottom horizontal edge of the lounger, then measure up from one end of the pencil line and mark the height of the backrest, subtracting the thickness of the slats. Now, about 16 in/40 cm from the foot end of the lounger, measure up from

the bottom horizontal line to the height you want for the bed of the lounger—mine is 16 in/40 cm—remembering to subtract the thickness of the slats. Draw a soft curve for the front of your lounger to this line, then continue this line along the length of the bed and up the backrest, as on your sketch, before finishing with another soft curve to level off when you reach the end.

Continued

2

TIPS

- **STEP 3** When you are satisfied with the shape you have drawn, get rid of any unwanted pencil lines by sanding them away with a sheet of 120-grit sandpaper. This will help avoid awkward mistakes when cutting with the saw.

- **STEP 4** Whole sheets of plywood are unruly and heavy things to maneuver, so try to get a helper to support the sheet during this part of the operation.

Before the cutting starts, check the jigsaw blade to be sure it won't cut through the supporting bench as it journeys around the board.

When using a jigsaw, always wear both safety goggles and a good-quality dust mask.

3 With the important line of the lounger scribed, you can now draw out the rest of the side section. In order to lighten the design, I decided to create a 3-in-/7.5-cm-tall opening at the bottom of the side section; it finishes in a tight curve, leaving a front and rear "foot" of 9¾ in/25 cm.

4 With the plywood marked up, it's time to cut out the first side section. Securely clamp the plywood in place. Using the jigsaw, follow your pencil marks to cut out the edges of the side section, along with the opening to create the feet.

5 Use the newly cut side section as a template to mark up the second side piece. Line it up with the remaining long edge on the plywood and use the pencil to transfer the shape. Clamp the plywood in place and then cut out the second side section with the jigsaw.

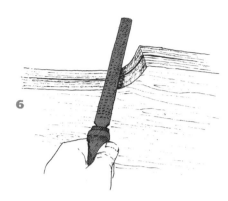

6 Align the side pieces and hold them together, using either clamps or securing them with two nails. This will keep both side sections even while you clean the edges with a wood rasp.

7 From the leftover plywood, measure and mark out five frame rails, making them 1½ in/4 cm shorter than the width you want your lounger to be to allow for the thickness of the side sections. I wanted a lounger 26 in/66 cm wide, so my rails were 6 by 24½ in/15 by 62 cm. On one rail, cut out an opening just as you did on the side sections, but this time only 1½ in/4 cm high. This will be the hand-hold for when the lounger needs to be moved into the sun's rays.

8 Using the handsaw, cut ten 6-in/15-cm battens from 1½-by-1½-in/4-by-4-cm boards and drill a pair of ³⁄₁₆-in/4-mm pilot holes on each end, staggered on adjacent faces.

9 Using the handsaw, cut two pieces of 2×2/5-by-5-cm board to fit inside the lounger feet at the back. Secure them with wood screws, then shape with a wood rasp to match the curve of the foot on the side section. These would give the feet on this end extra strength.

Continued

• **STEP 12** When securing
the second side section
to the rails, it's handy to
have a helper hold it in
place as you work.

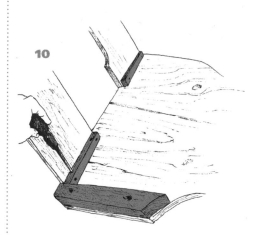

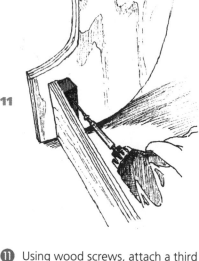

10 Next, you will be securing the
rails in place with wood screws driven
through the battens. Place one of the
side sections on the floor. Start with
the back rail with the hand-hold, and
position it flush to the top edge at the
back of the lounger. Directly below it,
attach another rail flush with the feet.

11 Using wood screws, attach a third
rail roughly at the center of the lounger
bed, flush with the top edge so that it
will sit just under the slats. Before you
attach the fourth rail at the foot end of
the lounger, raise it sufficiently from the
bottom to accommodate whatever you
have chosen as wheels.

12 The last rail is for the shelf, but first
attach a batten along its back edge to
prevent items from sliding off the edge.
Measure and mark the 1½-by-1½-in/
4-by-4-cm board to the same length as
the rail, cut with the handsaw, and nail
and glue in place. Now, using wood
screws, secure the shelf in place on top
of and at right angles to the rail that
will be at the bottom of the back. With
all five rails secured to the first side
section, place the second side section
in position on top of the rails and fasten
with wood screws.

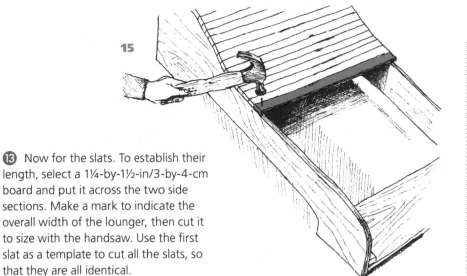

15

13 Now for the slats. To establish their length, select a 1¼-by-1½-in/3-by-4-cm board and put it across the two side sections. Make a mark to indicate the overall width of the lounger, then cut it to size with the handsaw. Use the first slat as a template to cut all the slats, so that they are all identical.

14 Remove any ragged edges from the slats and lounger frame with some sheets of 120-grit sandpaper. However, if you have decided to paint or varnish the sun lounger, now is a good time to apply it. With the slats unfitted, it will be far easier to apply.

15 With your finish of choice applied and dried, start from the top of the head end of the lounger and secure the slats into place with nails.

TIPS

• **STEP 13** The slats in my sun lounger are flush with the side sections, but you can make your slats overhang for a different look.

Using the pencil, write TEMPLATE on the template. Believe me, I know how easy it is to mistakenly pick up a scrap piece of wood and proceed to cut all of your components to the wrong size.

• **STEP 14** You can finish the slats with a wood stain that contrasts to the frame. Alternatively, a striking color in an exterior-grade paint could make more of a bold statement.

16 Attach two pairs of wheels to the rail at the front end of the lounger. Now, using the hand-hold rail, lift up the back end and roll it into the sun. Pour a cold drink, put on your shades, and test your work— I would recommend at least two hours for this.

16

The completed sun lounger.

(A) *The two feet at the back provide extra strength to help protect the side sections.* **(B)** *The rails help provide extra support for the lounger, and fitting them in place with the battens means the slats can sit flush with the side sections.* **(C)** *Position the wheels so they stay out of sight underneath the lounger.* **(D)** *The batten on the shelf prevents items from falling inside the lounger.* **(E)** *Keep the slats close together to form a smooth bed.* **(F)** *The slats are narrow so they can easily fit around the tight curves at the foot and head of the lounger.*

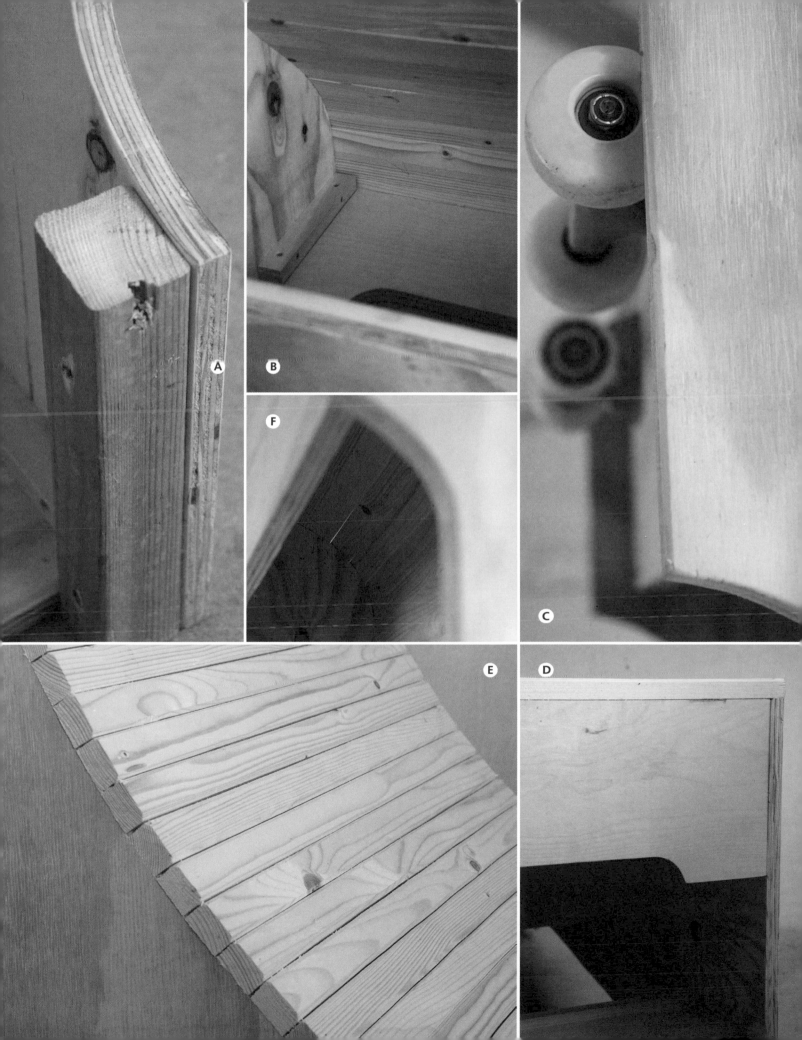

INDEX